PENGUIN CANADA

WHERE RACE DOES NOT MATTER

CECIL FOSTER is the author of several acclaimed works of fiction and non-fiction, including *No Man in the House*, *A Place Called Heaven*, *Sleep On Beloved*, and *Slammin' Tar*. Currently an assistant professor at the University of Guelph, Foster is also one of Canada's leading public intellectuals on issues of citizenship, culture, politics, race, ethnicity, multiculturalism, and immigration. He lives in Rockwood, Ontario.

Also by Cecil Foster

WHERE RACE DOES NOT MATTER

The New Spirit of Modernity

Cecil FOSTER

PENGUIN
CANADA

PENGUIN CANADA

Published by the Penguin Group

Penguin Group (Canada), 10 Alcorn Avenue, Toronto, Ontario, Canada M4V 3B2
(a division of Pearson Penguin Canada Inc.)

Penguin Group (USA) Inc., 375 Hudson Street, New York, New York 10014, U.S.A.
Penguin Books Ltd, 80 Strand, London WC2R 0RL, England
Penguin Ireland, 25 St Stephen's Green, Dublin 2, Ireland (a division of Penguin Books Ltd)
Penguin Group (Australia), 250 Camberwell Road, Camberwell, Victoria 3124, Australia
(a division of Pearson Australia Group Pty Ltd)
Penguin Books India Pvt Ltd, 11 Community Centre, Panchsheel Park, New Delhi – 110 017, India
Penguin Group (NZ), Cnr Airborne and Rosedale Roads, Albany, Auckland, New Zealand
(a division of Pearson New Zealand Ltd)
Penguin Books (South Africa) (Pty) Ltd, 24 Sturdee Avenue, Rosebank, Johannesburg 2196, South Africa

Penguin Books Ltd, Registered Offices: 80 Strand, London WC2R 0RL, England

First published 2005

1 2 3 4 5 6 7 8 9 10 (WEB)

Copyright © Cecil Foster, 2005

Author representation: Westwood Creative Artists
94 Harbord Street, Toronto, Ontario M5S 1G6

Excerpts from the following sources are reproduced with kind permission. Pages 46, 47–48: The speeches of Sir J. Percy Fitzpatrick and Dr. George P. Gilmour courtesy of The Empire Club of Canada. Pages 90–91: *The Philadelphia Negro: A Social Study* by W. E. B. Du Bois courtesy of the University of Pennsylvania Press. Page 99: *Citizen Plus: Aboriginal People of Canada and the Canadian State* by Alan C. Cairns reproduced with the permission of the publisher © University of British Columbia Press, 2000. All rights reserved by the publisher. Pages 127, 128, 131, 132, 133, 135: *My Vision of Canada* by William Arthur Deacon courtesy of Mary E. Haines. Page 141: "A Black Man Talks about Race Prejudice in White Canada" by Austin Clarke from the April 23, 1963, issue of *Maclean's* magazine courtesy of Austin Clarke. Pages 147–148: *Diversity, Mobility, and Social Change: The Dynamics of Black Communities in Canada* courtesy of James L. Torczyner. Pages 166, 169, 173, 175: *The Essential Trudeau* by Ron Graham courtesy of Ron Graham and the Trudeau Foundation. Pages 182, 183: *Odysseys Home* by George Elliott Clarke courtesy of the University of Toronto Press.

Manufactured in Canada.

LIBRARY AND ARCHIVES CANADA CATALOGUING IN PUBLICATION

Foster, Cecil, 1954–
Where race does not matter : the new spirit of modernity / Cecil Foster.

Includes bibliographical references and index.
ISBN 0-14-301769-1

1. Race relations—History. 2. Racism—History. 3. National state.
I. Title.

HT1507.F68   2005   305.8'009   C2004-905383-3

Visit the Penguin Group (Canada) website at **www.penguin.ca**

To

Christene Michelle
&
Mensah Kafele

For giving love
... and hope

Holla Back!

For Raphael
Who picked me up

CONTENTS

PREFACE

I n many respects, this book is a conversation. It is also a reflection. And it is an idealist dream, perhaps falling just short of a utopian one. I hope this book allows us to think about not only our current existence but also all that we have overcome and can still hope to achieve. Most of all, it is my way of coming to terms with myself as a Black Canadian, and as an immigrant who feels blessed to be living in Canada at this time yet can imagine a society in which all citizens are genuinely equal and share the same rights and privileges. That is what I call genuine multiculturalism—for ultimately multiculturalism is about hope, dreams, idealism, and grasping for what is now beyond reach. That is the legacy left us by Prime Minister Pierre Trudeau. And yet multiculturalism is more than just rights, privileges, legacies, and even the politics of recognition; it is also the hope that all humanity—with its differences and diversity—can look to a future in which every individual will be treated as someone of value and worth, as part of a community of his or her choosing, and ultimately as part of the only race that matters, the human race. Multiculturalism is about living and about the aspirations of the living. It is a dream not just about Canada but about Canada's gift and, ultimately, its legacy to the world.

But multiculturalism is also about memory—in this specific case, a shared history in this place called Canada. That this is a shared history is for many people ironic. Indeed, it is also paradoxical.

For a long moment in Canada's existence, the dominant view was that Canada was not to be shared by the peoples of the world. Canada was meant to be a place set aside for a specific and narrowly defined group or *race* of people. These people were exclusively the descendants of Western Europeans. All others, including those aboriginal to the land, were to be excluded. Those from the excluded groups that maintained a presence within Canada were to be marginalized and classified as inferior. Such was the official dogma, the religion of nation-state formation. This is a memory of hatred and terror and dehumanization for those on the outside. It is also the story of privilege for the few on the inside. All these experiences put together amount to a chapter in the chronology of disillusionment for so many and a history of the Americas. Still, this is the narrative of the hope that triumphs over despair and the spirit that just would not die.

In our reflections we must retell this story, for in the retelling we not only keep a memory alive, we also remember those who lost opportunities and those who fought for a different way of existence. In retelling these stories, perhaps we that live in another time might be able to spot those virulent strains of racism that seem neither to disappear entirely nor to remain underground for very long. In the retelling, we remember all those who suffered but who never lost hope, and whose admonition to us is simply "to learn the young'uns" and never to forget. In the retelling, we hold up as paragons of justice those who chose to be different. We hold dear a country that finally chose idealistically, for the good of all humanity, to be different from all others in the Americas. In this retelling, we name what was and still is evil, while holding up the good.

Indeed, in our collective memory that is our history of sharing a land together, a Canada exists of which the majority of us are not proud. It is partly because of this shame that we collectively looked at the terror of a racialized state and turned our backs on it. This is the memory of the moment that gave multiculturalism its birth—

a moment that gave not only Canada but the entire Americas and the world something that was new, fresh, and full of hope. In that moment what we now know to be good was born. In retelling, therefore, we are always celebrating a new birth. For something good happens each time we remember and share our memories. We are venerating all those who chose a different path and who can now be counted among the stalwarts that sacrificed themselves for a specific kind of freedom that is multiculturalism. It is because the country has changed that some of us would rather we forget and converse only about the good and the beautiful. But can we possibly talk about the good and beautiful without also acknowledging the evil? By not retelling the entire story, we run the risk of forgetting that multiculturalism was a difficult decision and that not everyone chose this path. We would also be forgetting that history is about discontinuities as well.

In relating these stories, we take the baton from those who have carried the quest so far. We join them in the onward march towards what was once considered not only unthinkable but decidedly unacceptable in the days when choices were being made and a different vision dominated. Now what we consider to be unacceptable is that any of the old visions of exclusion should still linger among us. In this way, by telling ourselves these stories, we recognize how far we have come, while also recognizing that there is a ways to go—either to wipe out what is left of the discredited vision or to achieve what is now our new hope and aspiration. And in doing all this, we keep talking and reflecting and dreaming anew. We keep sharing our stories that, in the end, amount to just one story with many versions. Here is the version that I want to tell: a new spirit is among us, a spirit that, paradoxically, is as old as humanity, a spirit that is a spectre or shade equally of another time and of conflicting dreams and choices. It is a story that, ironically, is also about a new spirit of modernity. Multiculturalism is the story of our search for and hopes about social justice.

And I make these claims because I think race and ethnicity are still serious issues facing us. But just as importantly, there is now an opening in history that is available to us. This opportunity allows us to dream of what so many people would have thought impossible—a place and time where race genuinely does not matter.

chapter one

THE MORALITY OF HISTORY

There has never been a time in the history of nations when race did not matter. Perhaps we are reaching the point where the same can no longer be said for skin colour. Such an achievement would be momentous enough to merit yet another declaration that a history has ended—this time a history of what we call race.

"Let us hurry to untie the knot and set the good genius of European civilisation once more free from the bonds which may strangle her in the future."[1] These were the inspirational words of one of South Africa's—and, by extension, Europe's—leading statesmen of the early twentieth century, Jan Christiaan Smuts. Presenting himself as an oracle in the ancient Greek tragedian tradition, the sixty-four-year-old Smuts was at the height of his international fame when he made these comments in the fall of 1934. He had identified a single purpose of human existence, the attainment of different levels of culture and "civilization" by different groups, and he was sharing it with those whom he felt most likely to bring about the ending he thought so necessary for humanity. Smuts spoke with great passion and fanfare, as he was prone to do when discussing world affairs, especially before European audiences.

Europe, he believed, was the key to unlocking a world of perpetual peace.

Smuts spoke in a time of acute tensions in international affairs. Storm clouds were building everywhere. Nations, and even individual groups within nations, were erecting protective barriers around themselves. The best example of this for Smuts was Germany, which had withdrawn into itself and cloaked its affairs in mystery, something that he thought separated it from its natural heritage as a European nation. This was another treacherous moment for the era that we call Modernity: the period that stretches from the present day back to the end of the so-called Middle Ages that is generally associated in world history with the assertion of the identity and culture of the individual, or self, as a unified whole and with what is called development and progress. This era reached its idealized apex with the affirmation of the individual person as the highest form of attainment in a liberal democracy. At the global level, it reached its pinnacle with the formation of nation-states with supposedly clear identities and cultures that are separate from the rest of humanity. These are the times of the idealized individual, either as a unique personality or as a distinct collective or people.

At the start of the twentieth century, the spirit among these nation-states was foul, as increasingly they were segregating themselves into teams of "us" and "them" as part of a global fight for personal and universal dominance. The awareness that flowed out of this identity and culture, and that might very well be considered separate from the entity itself, is what I shall be calling the spirit of Modernity. Put another way, it is the purported soul, or the consciousness, of the individual or the collective unity. Spirit, as an expression—especially as captured in institutions, practices, and common agencies as part of the prevailing ideology—is that cultural or social bond that allows the many individuals in a society to think, act, and dream as a collective.

On Smuts's mind in particular was Adolf Hitler, who, in his attempt to devise a new world order, would unleash from his Pandora's box some of the worst curses that have ever been visited upon us. These pestilences were packaged under the banner of race and ultimately were symbolized as moral evils by the words "Auschwitz" and "the Holocaust." They were a direct outcrop of Modernity's love affair with the prototypical individual with a distinct identity and culture. At the specific moment of his speech, in 1934, Smuts was arguing that there was still hope. If the major powers of the world treated Hitler fairly, lessening the economic burdens that had been imposed on Germany at the end of the First World War, then there would be less reason for all Germans to feel constrained by forces over which they had no control. They would no longer feel unnaturally restrained from their purported rendezvous with destiny. This way, Smuts argued, Hitler and the German people were unlikely to see themselves as inferior in treatment and unfairly positioned on the international stage.

"How can the inferiority complex which is obsessing and, I fear, poisoning the mind, and indeed the very soul, of Germany be removed?" Smuts asked. He believed that all of Europe, and there-fore civilization in general, was caught in the grips of separate and competing complexes caused by fear of war and by inferiority hang-ups. Both obsessions, he said, could lead to war by forcing different states and people to confront one another to lessen their fears. These were complexes that rose up from deep within the dark consciousness of Europeans—a casting back to primitive, child-like concerns—and that psychologically would have to be dealt with in a mature and civil manner. "There is only one way, [and] that is to recognize her [Germany's] complete equality of status with her fellows, and to do so frankly, freely and unreservedly. That is the only medicine for her disease. And when we have summoned up sufficient courage to treat her in that human way, as our equal in the comity of nations, then, and not till then, will the old wound cease to fester and poison the life of Europe and the world."[2]

As Smuts saw it, Hitler and the defeated forces of the previous war, if treated fairly, would be less likely to fight for their dignity and to assert not only their equality but their superiority as a European people. In one sense, what Smuts was saying was old: he was one of the few international figures who had refused to be a signatory to the conditions imposed on Germany after the First World War. He had argued, at the International Peace Conference at Versailles in 1919, that harsh economic sanctions would lead to underdevelopment in Europe and possibly to another major conflagration. (Germany's obligations included reparation payments to the Allied nations for the economic damage caused by the war.) But in another sense, what he was saying was different: he was offering a specific policy for a new world order, one that bound together all of Europe, and its previous and remaining colonies and outposts worldwide, as one unit with one purpose in life. Europeans would occupy a position of superiority in this new world order. The main distinctive markers of this group's members would be, culturally, their European heritage and sensibilities, their Christian religion, and, ultimately and biologically, the whiteness of their skin colour.

Smuts was talking about the formulation of a single foreign policy that would be the cornerstone of a universal approach to this emerging new order. This policy would capture what little hope Smuts thought still existed in international affairs. It was to be an approach to international behaviour, and places like Canada, Australia, New Zealand, and South Africa—in effect, Europeans living off the continent of Europe—would have input and were expected to be in agreement. These favoured countries were to help formulate this policy, even if it was to be carried out primarily by officials in London and in the name of what Smuts saw as the greatest achievement of identity and culture in history, the British Empire.

For Smuts, a fractured approach to world affairs had taken root in Europe and the Far East. Everywhere, people appeared to be giving up on the much-cherished League of Nations, an organization that Smuts and the American president Woodrow Wilson had brought forth out of the ashes of the first great war. The League of Nations had been hamstrung by parochial differences, and even tribalism, and it seemed unable to meet its unwritten mandate to prevent another world war. Although he was a South African Afrikaner by birth, Smuts had no doubt who he really was racially: as much a European as if he had been born on the continent. He claimed as a legacy what he called the greatest civilization in history. He was as European as any other official from elsewhere in the British Empire, particularly those in Canada, Australia, and New Zealand who'd helped to formulate British policy both on the European continent and in what was viewed, from the perspective of these Europhiles, as the netherworld of colonies and of primitiveness.

Everywhere he looked in the world, Smuts saw bleakness and despair and despondency. On that particular day, as he gave his speech on world affairs, he was also feeling the chill of an oncoming global conflagration that, exactly as he prophesied, would claim millions of people the world over in a seemingly mindless frenzy. This was a dangerous illness, Smuts warned, one that could lead to the destruction of humanity. It was also proof that world leaders had not learned the lessons of the past. Unless the correct psychoanalytic diagnosis was made and the great peoples of Europe were redirected from the wrong course, they were destined, Smuts thought, to repeat history with all its gore.

As an alternative, Smuts offered a part of his grand design for the world, a scheme that was based on conquering the inherent primitiveness in nature and in individuals. His solution was predicated on the recognition of the centrality of diversity and difference, along with the concomitant realization that difference and diversity in humanity made some groups of people superior and others inferior. In other words, Smuts's design to save the world was founded on the elevation of race, and race was ultimately reduced to the colour of the skin, ethnic background, and culture. For him, hierarchical differences could occur even within the oneness that is humanity, a League of Nations, the British Empire, or a nation-state. Race demanded that differences based on purported natural superiority and inferiority be separated out and respected. Race was supposedly the glue of nation-states, linking the same type of people in a unity, and it was to be found everywhere.

Smuts's argument to that world-famous institute in London was that the Second World War was not as inevitable as it first appeared, and that a return to justice in human affairs might yet spare the world the chaos and slaughter of another major war. Like an oracle, he presented himself as someone who could read the entrails of history to make greater sense of the present. Like a prophet, he could surmise future outcomes from present condi-tions, making allowances for a series of actions or refusals to act. Smuts's contention was that humanity needed to return to the basics of civility, to justice and generosity towards the weak and defeated, and to those tropes of Christian charity and grace on which the great European civilization was built. In his view, this civilization was the finest achievement in history, and one that separated Europeans from all other races and their civilizations the world over. But he also believed this European civilization was as flawed as it was great. It had produced countless technological advances and improvements in the human condition, as well as many internecine wars that served only to undermine its greatness and its goal of advancing the human condition.

Implying that the leading Europeans of the day were missing the point behind the drive to war, Smuts suggested that they needed "to recognize that it [the impulse towards war] is a disease and not a healthy condition." Smuts presented himself as the psychoanalyst that Europe needed. "Once Europeans admit to themselves that they are perhaps a little mad," he asserted, "the cure will come itself. A sense of humour, of good humour, and a little laughter at themselves will do the rest. 'Know thyself,' said the wise oracle. 'Know thyself' is the word to be spoken to Europe today in its temporary obsessions and aberrations."[3]

The answer was for Europe to recognize both its greatness and its psychosis, and for it not to take itself so seriously as to become blinded by its own follies and human frailties. If it did this, Europe would be able to pick itself up off the psychoanalytic couch and take the steps needed to maintain its leadership and moral superiority in the world. For Smuts, the world order and race were issues of the mind and, in the final analysis, morality, not only biology or culture. As it did for the ancient Greek tragedian heroes, the answer rested first in knowing good and evil, and even in recognizing the good and evil that is within. Race was moral well-being.

Of course, the scheme that Smuts was offering to the world was captured in words that could only harm those who were left out of it. His statements were intended to divide humanity into at least two groups: a superior civilization of elite nations from Europe, and those who were inferior both in the roles they would play on the international stage and in the human quest for freedom. As history shows, Smuts's prophesy did not save Europe from another slaughter; the Second World War started just over four years after his speech, and it culminated in a holocaust premised, ironically, on the same notion of race that he had thought could save Europe.

Smuts would probably have argued that, as happened with the League of Nations, nobody listened to him. But he was a leading actor in global politics, and he did play a role in how the world was divided up among the prevailing powers after the First World War. The new world order he helped to create almost made this new round of depravity possible. As many students of Western civilization would later argue, the killing fields and gas chambers of the

Second World War were unavoidably the natural conclusion to that same civilization, especially when viewed from a Eurocentric perspective. They would argue that this responsibility or ownership rested with the thinking it produced, and that the thinking in turn produced the civilization that Smuts so venerated. He saw a kind of greatness, a self-imposed white man's task, that he wanted Europeans to maintain and project on all humanity. But devastation and inhumanity were the real results of Smuts's thinking. His belief that the world could be made to suit the purposes of a specific group of people who supposedly constituted a separate and more privileged race failed to recognize that in most cases the world has a purpose of its own, and that history is amoral enough to move however it likes, not according to the wishes and desires of any person or group. Indeed, history unfurls as it should, and as it pleases. In this sense, history was anti-Modernity: if there was to be unity, it would be a fractured one; its distinctiveness would be its fragmentation.

But at their core, Smuts's plans aimed for the redemption of humanity, or at least a specific branch, or race, of it. Words with the same intended effect came from a man who was seemingly excluded from Smuts's design, a man who in many ways was the opposite of Smuts himself. These words had echoed in London's cavernous but nearly empty Royal Albert Hall on a late-spring night on June 6, 1928: "The cry is raised all over the world today of Canada for the Canadians, of America for the Americans, of England for the English, of France for the French, of Germany for the Germans. Do you think it unreasonable that we, the Blacks of the world, should raise the cry of Africa for the Africans?"[4]

So said the Black cosmopolitan citizen Marcus Mosiah (Mose) Garvey, in an address to a mere two hundred people at an event that he had put on at great personal financial cost, and on which he had been pinning his hopes for personal redemption. His words gave voice to a view held by millions of people living in the nether-

8

world that was not European in its aspirations but was associated with the stings and worthlessness of colonialism and imperialism, and with presumed primitiveness and racial inferiority.

The Jamaican-born visionary Garvey was viewed, by whites and Blacks alike, as one of the greatest products of the so-called Black race and civilization. He spoke on the international stage with an authority unknown at that time to many people of African heritage, an authority that he claimed had leaders of white countries conspiring to brand him a thief and an embezzler. While Smuts was white, Garvey was Black. While Smuts was educated at or honoured by world-renowned universities, Garvey was self-taught. Just as Smuts believed he was European even though he was not born in Europe, Garvey believed he was African even though he was not born in Africa. Smuts represented the so-called European civilization and Garvey the African version—and both men argued, for different reasons, that it was not natural to mix the two. Smuts spoke both for and from the centre of power and the dominant world order in the British Empire; Garvey spoke to the centre of power, but he did it from the periphery.

The forty-eight-year-old Garvey had much riding on his speech that day. He was hoping for a personal upliftment following the fall from grace he suffered when he was falsely imprisoned in the United States for fraud. Deemed an undesirable alien, he was deported to his native Jamaica, an island still administered by colonial rule at a time when the more affluent members of the British Empire had attained responsible government and were in charge of at least their own domestic affairs. Garvey used the speech to argue that even though he was once a prisoner, he was not a crook, and that he had no evil intentions towards anyone, particularly anyone of the white race. It was the United States and its policies towards Blacks—policies that got him imprisoned on false charges—that were corrupt and evil. These policies, he said, existed because the United States was founded on the unnatural mixing and exploiting of races, an experiment that, among the many other things that aggrieved Africans, had produced a "mongrel population" of nearly four hundred thousand people. This aggravation, Garvey suggested, was on top of the universal dehumanizing of Africans.

Noted for his eloquence and his ability to mobilize people across national and state lines, Garvey was the leader of the New York–based Universal Negro Improvement Association (UNIA), an organization that at its height represented eleven million Blacks and Africans around the world. Garvey fought for justice for Blacks and Africans the world over, but his ultimate goal was the *creation* of a "natural" homeland for them in Africa. This homeland, the United States of Black Africa, was the main plank of Garvey's and UNIA's orthodoxy. This was where the Modernist ideal of a single and unified identity for all Black people was to take root. In this homeland, the differences among Black people were to be assimilated into a racialized unity, producing sameness in all members. This uniformity of identity and culture would stand in opposition to its Other, an alternative uniformity of identity and culture in a civilization of Europe and Europeans living abroad, as dreamt of by Smuts and thinkers like him.

"We believe in the freedom of Africa for the Negro people of the world, and by the principle of Europe for the Europeans and Asia for the Asiatics, we demand Africa for the Africans at home and abroad,"[5] wrote Garvey in the Declaration of Rights of the Negro Peoples of the World, a manifesto drawn up by the 122 delegates to the first International Convention of the UNIA, held at Liberty Hall in New York City in 1920. The convention was the equivalent of a Black League of Nations, and it met, at Garvey's calling, for the entire month of August, drawing up what amounted to a treaty governing the treatment of Blacks living in white countries and a constitution for the Black homeland in Africa. In the manifesto, intended to bring dignity to Blacks and Africans the world over, Garvey proposed human and social prototypes that were the opposites of Smuts's but produced by the same methods. His aim was not to make the case for what we would now call reparations for slavery and colonialism, but to create a United States of Black Africa on any part of the African continent that the white *race* was willing to surrender to Garvey and his group.

In the Royal Albert Hall speech, offered by a fallen Garvey to a sprinkling of liberal-minded English citizens, he once again asserted that the world would be a better place if what he called the Black, white, red, and yellow races respected each other but lived apart in homelands that would provide the natural environments for the perfecting of each race. In their separate homelands, the races could establish their own institutions and agencies to create distinct cultures and civilizations. This was the pre-eminent message of the man who was widely known as the Black Moses or the Black Messiah, a man whose parents knew, even at his birth, that he should be named for one of two great men of history— Moses of the Bible or Marcus Aurelius, the famous Roman emperor.

Garvey also related in this pivotal speech the mythology of Europe's proud history, of a proud people who produced their own distinct civilization and culture. But from his perspective, this was a story with a twist. To Garvey, the narrative of European civilization was also a tale of inhuman suffering endured by Black people; it was the story of how they were taken out of Africa as slaves, of how Blacks and Africans had provided the sweat and labour that built the very civilization that Smuts found so great, and of how they were denied the opportunity to produce a great civilization of their own.

It was for this reason that Garvey had assembled a group of Black and African intellectuals under the banner of his UNIA to make the case for a Black nation-state. "We are 280 million homeless people, without a country and no flag," he asserted. "In America they make a joke of it that every nation has a flag but the coon. You will find that in mimicry and in song."[6] By resorting to this hateful and self-deprecating language, specifically by using the word "coon," Garvey was showing that he was not speaking from a position of strength. Unlike Smuts, he was not part of the power elite speaking to itself. Instead, he was projecting an image of inferiority and powerlessness, begging for the mercy and charity of an established group of superior beings. Flattering his London audience, Garvey declared that the Anglo-Saxons of England were more moral and just than the Anglo-Americans and others of the white race, and that he was appealing to the Anglo-Saxon race's innate and natural sense of fairness and love of justice. He also allowed that he was willing to take, for his proposed homeland in Africa, any territory that England, France, Belgium, Portugal, Germany, Italy, or any other European master was willing to give up.

"Tonight," Garvey said, driving home his appeal for justice and separation, "we have on the platform here native sons of Africa, descendants of slaves in the western world, Negroes of America and Negroes from the West Indies. We have come to tell you how we feel about it [the history of Black and African civilization] and what we want done at the present time to prevent a recurrence of what happened to us hundreds of years ago."[7] Modern-day Garveys may be calling for economic redress, in the form of reparations payments, for the same wrongs discussed by the UNIA leader, but Garvey, addressing a crowd that was disappointingly small, was content to settle for an acknowledgment of the misdeeds done, and for the granting of lands in Africa so that, as a race, Blacks and Africans could mark the end of one history and the beginning of another. This was his great design. But try as he might, Garvey could not hide that he'd been reduced to begging the European powers to give him a bit of land in Africa to resuscitate his dream for African people. Absent was the dignity that Garvey and his people had hoped would back their demands, on behalf of all Blacks and Africans, for justice, for fairness, and for the righteousness of their cause. On that night, nobody of note apparently listened to this voice in the wilderness of human affairs.

Garvey left London empty-handed, with his own words about the exclusion of Blacks from Western society ringing in his ears. "In your respective countries you do not want us," he had said, continuing his plea for a place where Blacks would be wanted, where they would be able to make a living for themselves, becoming their own statesmen, artists, and scientists. A place where Blacks and Africans would no longer be a bother or a charge on the consciences of whites. No longer a burden or a task for the white man. "We cannot go to Australia and get a living; we cannot go to Canada and get a living; we cannot come to England and get a living; you will not employ us." In this sense, Garvey was like the blind king of classical Greek tragedy, unintentionally foretelling a fate for himself that even he could not avoid or change.

At the end of September 1928, Garvey left England for his home in Jamaica, travelling by way of Canada, Bermuda, and the Bahamas. When he arrived in Montreal, his first stop across the Atlantic, he was arrested for entering the country illegally. After some embarrassment and humiliation for both Garvey and the authorities, he was released, for technically he was not only a Jamaican but also a British subject, and that gave him the right to travel to and live in any part of the British Empire, a commonwealth of which Canada and Jamaica were supposedly equal members. Obviously, Canadian authorities did not see things that way; nor did they practise this equality of rights for all British subjects. As his biographer, John Henrik Clarke, asserts, Garvey's detention was clearly intended to humiliate him. The white authorities who administered Bermuda also refused to let him in, although he was allowed to address a meeting of followers in the Bahamas.

To the critical eye, it might appear as if Garvey and Smuts were preaching from different pulpits, even if they occasionally used the same platforms. But in truth, they were simply holding different ends of the same strand of thought. They were worshipping the same ideal as they endeavoured to make happen in the real world what they knew only in their minds. Their aim was to refashion their own societies, and international relations in general, according to this faith. The results of their thinking were profound: both men elevated race to the status of official state policy.

Race had become the desideratum for happiness at home and abroad. Around the world, several high-profile people in the arenas of politics, religion, economics, and academia held opinions similar to those of Smuts and Garvey. For them, race was part of a natural order. This was an idea that had wide currency, especially among those with a social Darwinian bent. They believed that to attain their highest levels, societies had to separate into clear and distinct groups of superior and inferior people with their own identities and cultures.

To this way of thinking, all men and women were not created equal. Some were like an inferior subspecies, possessed of the minimum abilities, virtues, and aptitudes that it took to be human. Others were near-perfect specimens, hovering on the threshold of achieving the mythical greatness of gods. In Canada, we saw such thinking espoused by the political leaders of the day, including Sir Wilfrid Laurier and Mackenzie King, and even by socialist leaders like Tommy Douglas. All of these men, writes Angus McLaren in his book *Our Own Master Race,* at different times supported an officially sanctioned exercise in eugenics that continued until at least 1945.[8] The aim of the program was to breed a master race of Canadians by weeding out what were considered to be undesirable traits in some humans. The idea was to produce a specific type of human being by adopting the same methods that were used to produce types of horses, dogs, and cattle, as well as varieties of grains and apples. The social engineers behind the program tried, for example, to sterilize people who were deemed to be mentally and physically handicapped, thereby controlling who was allowed to have children and pass on genes to future generations. The program was even at the heart of an immigration policy that aimed to select the "right" groups of people. When mixed together or combined with the Canadian environment, the selected people were supposed to produce, in a short period of time, an elite Canadian specimen with the characteristics and virtues that the leaders of the experiment felt were important. Race was at the heart of it all, and the plan called for undesirable types, or races, of people—all but Western Europeans, that is—to be kept out of Canada. This would eliminate the possibility of their passing their supposedly inferior genes into the superior races in Canada.

In the United States, as the historians Francis D. Adams and Barry Sanders show in *Alienable Rights: The Exclusion of African Americans in a White Man's Land,* it is to this day impossible to find a president whose views on public policy have not been shaped by race. This was traditionally even the case in literature and the arts, areas heavily populated with followers of, for example, Rudyard Kipling, whose belief that Europeans were superior to other peoples of the world played a key role in shaping thought in the British Empire. We can think as well of the poet Ezra Pound and his anti-Semitism, and, at the other extreme, of Paul Robeson fighting anti-Black racism. And as we shall see, these times were also influenced by people like the American sociologist and civil rights leader W. E. B. Du Bois, who had argued from the beginning that the main battles of the twentieth century would be fought across the colour line. This was a view echoed by the Canadian prime minister Wilfrid Laurier, but for a quite different reason. For Laurier, the century would bring glory to Canada on the domestic and international stages primarily because the country was going to maintain the colour line that Du Bois wanted erased.

Another person whose views had international reach was Cecil Rhodes, an English-born South African and former prime minister of the Cape Colony, who endowed the scholarships that bear his name and allow outstanding students from around the world to study at Oxford University. Rhodes had dreamed of painting the map of Africa, from the Cape to Cairo, British red as a testament to the superiority of European and British cultures. The legacy he left to Oxford University came partly from the exploitation of African labour in what was then called Rhodesia and South Africa. As leading luminaries in the British Empire, Kipling and Rhodes and others like them helped shape world opinion, including views in Canada, on the appropriate order for social development at home, elsewhere in the British Empire, and wider afield.

Their elevation of race to national and international prominence was an approach that informed most of the past century and still hangs over the world today. Many decades would pass before the world was able to dismantle this policy of officially dividing humanity into racialized groups. The civilization firing Smuts's imagination was simply European and white. This was the ideal, the highest level of attainment, the prototype to which everything in human life was to conform.

In his quest to build a better world, Smuts often boasted about the new spirit that he and others were creating in South Africa. This, he averred, was where the experiment would produce the desired results. Such chest-thumping was on the agenda on March 22, 1935, when Smuts addressed the mainly white delegates to the Imperial Press Conference in Cape Town. He used the occasion to tell the international journalists of the new spirit of his new nation, a land that had once been no more than African savannah. The journalists, he said, would now see "not only natives and game, but also the type of European we are breeding in this new country and the standard of civilisation we are trying to uphold under the difficult conditions in Africa."[9] On this foundation, he would build an idealistic society imbued with a new and different type of spirit.

Smuts invited the journalists to share with the rest of the world the unique human experiment that was then emerging in South Africa. "You will now go back to your own great countries, with most of which South Africa cannot for a moment hope to bear comparison," he told them. "You will see again the green hills of the British Isles and the great cities with their teeming millions and high civilisation; you will see again Canada and Australia, with their endless wheat fields, and New Zealand, the gem, I am told, of the Commonwealth. But in all that grandeur of your home countries you will think back to this strange, primitive land, its curious history, its unique physical features, its flora and fauna found nowhere else, its human races ranging from the very lowest to the highest, its dark problems, some of the hardest ever offered to us humans to solve." Smuts hoped that images of South Africa would resonate with the journalists and their audience for a long time. "At a distance and in retrospect you will sometimes think of South Africa, and its strange fascinations, attractive to some, repellent to others. You will try to picture its unknown past, and you will perhaps speculate on its future, on what fate has in store for this country and its great human experiment."[10] Indeed, Smuts's images of progress and degeneracy, of civilization and primitivism, and of whiteness and Blackness were the same whether he was talking about the need for international peace or the mission to create a new "natural" order in his own country. His dreams did not change, even though the audiences for his speeches did. To them all, he offered a message about the sanctity of race.

As far back as May 22, 1917, in a speech delivered at London's Savoy Hotel, Smuts had begun promoting the so-called white man's task, the principles of an overriding policy towards South Africa's native peoples. Some of these beliefs, which he called the emerging South African spirit, would eventually find their way into the country's official policies on race. What he intended as an example to the entire world became the foundations of apartheid South Africa.

Smuts's blueprint—his ideas of what should be done and what mistakes should be avoided—was drawn from the experiences of Canada, especially the way it handled its Native problem, its attempts to "breed" a new human specimen in a land that used to be "primitive," and its struggles to create a new Canadian spirit by bonding two European cultures, the English and the French. The new South Africa would succeed where Canada had failed, producing one unified race out of two European ethnicities. The aim in South Africa was for the Dutch and the English to overcome the differences that had thus far kept them in a perpetual state of war. The problem, according to Smuts, was that they had foolishly and unthinkingly sought to preserve separate languages, traditions, and "national" types within the same nation-state. White South Africans had to overcome the fear that their particular European identity and culture would be "swallowed up and ... submerged" by a new national identity and culture that was a hybrid of the two older ones. Smuts even criticized those South Africans who "point to the precedent of Canada, where French-Canadians are also standing aside [in isolation] from the general current of Canadian life and national development for the same reason [given above]. Now, you know, that is the issue which is being fought out now in South Africa, and has been fought out in recent years more acutely than ever before."[11]

The new spirit, for Smuts, would see different people, operating for their own good and out of their best interests, take separate and distinct paths to different endings. In no small way, race had fully and concretely come into its own as a national and an international policy. More so than in the past, the world was tied in a big knot. Both Smuts and Garvey looked to Africa as a cradle of civilization, the birthplace of all humanity, but Smuts placed native-born Africans on the same level as the big game on display for hunters and tourists. For Garvey, Africa was home for Africans, and no other group of people. With his shouts of "Africa for the Africans," he moved millions of people around the world and offered them a chance to claim their own distinct and separate homeland, culture, and civilization. His goal was the elevation of the Black race, and he was seeking to draw people from around the world back to a common homeland that was African, if not always in Africa. He was as much promoting a kind of apartheid as Smuts, except that in his model he chose to include the very people that Smuts and other nation builders rejected.

Smuts and Garvey—one was the yin to the other's yang. But both would leave an impact on our collective imagination and in the lives we still live; both would promote the ideas that freedom, happiness, and sufficiency could be found only within secured boundaries, and that progress came from living exclusively among one's own kind; both were marking out the terrain that would eventually host much of the debate and violence, including the genocides and exercises in ethnic cleansing, of the twenty-first century. Ultimately, for the good of humanity, both men and their ideas would have to be repudiated. Their morality, history would teach us, was all wrong. Unity is in diversity and difference, not in the erasing of them.

BUT FROM OUR VANTAGE POINT, that is supposedly all in the past. The present is before us, and official apartheid is history. The dream of Africans retaining Africa is enjoying a renaissance, and the continent is now viewed as the mythical homeland for all the peoples of the world. South Africa's president, Thabo Mbeki, a successor of both Smuts and Garvey, says this is a reclamation for all Africans, "both Black and white." Indeed, the preamble to the current Constitution of South Africa claims that "we, the people … believe that South Africa belongs to all who live in it, united in our diversity." Elsewhere around the globe, the talk is of inclusiveness, of inspiring people of allegedly different races to create out of themselves one people, mongrelized though they may be, and to fashion one ethnicity out of racial impurities. The talk is of multiculturalism, of a raceless state of affairs in a nation-state that is as much a diaspora as it is a homeland. Canada is the pioneer once again on this journey to a supposed utopia.

As we make what might be a pivotal turn in this freedom march, striding into what will perhaps emerge as raceless times, the question is, Have we magically found the elusive answer, a way of releasing the loop without having to sever the ends? If so, this would satisfy both the few and the many, the lords and the bondsmen. This would be a new world where race does not matter, either biologically or culturally, and where there are no hierarchies of types of individuals or groups, nations or states, cultures or civilizations. At the same time, the citizens of this new world would be trying to live out a national history with no clearly discernible outcomes, no ideals of perfection to which they must aspire. In this scenario, the future is open-ended; it's marked by diversity and not the acquisition of sameness.

Still, the question remains: Is it possible to have a nation-state or a country without race? Can we fully unmake the idol of Modernity and imbue it with a new spirit? I believe we must seize this moment of creation that is upon us and make it last for as long as possible, living in an eternal present, without a manmade ending and without a future scripted by a group of people acting from their own limited knowledge. We will live together in the here and now, building on our collective knowledge, making decisions and choices in accordance with the morality lessons we have learned. We will cease claiming that we are not now and have never been a special and unique people, that we are not now and will never be special and exclusive. We are a people without a race or an ideal of purity, a people who have more in common with the mongrelized population that Garvey had once termed a social aggravation. Our unity will be a composite made by taking a bit from here, there, and everywhere; it will not be a unity that is unalloyed and supposedly given to us by gods or nature.

This is the end to which, despite Smuts and Garvey and people like them, humanity in general has striven. This raceless place is the universal heaven of our mythologies. This is the meaning of the story of dispersal, of going forth and multiplying, of living in diasporas instead of homelands. It is a quest for a freedom that for the longest time we thought could be had only by retreating into our specific and distinct groups and living civilly together, and by sharing our risks and achievements in a nation or state that is homogeneous and without diversity.

All along, we thought we would be on easy street if we entered the homeland through the gates of the nation-state, and if we removed from beyond the walls of the city and the pale of history all who supposedly did not belong. Perhaps the problem was always with the state itself—although it certainly should not wither away. Indeed, the state has a role to play, administratively and as a rallying point of sorts. The problems with the current idea of the state lie with the way we select the materials, with what types of materials we want, and with the way we try to build it. There is a problem with how the state is imagined. We need to turn it on its head, challenging assumptions of what is necessary for a united, happy, and self-sufficient society, and also re-evaluating how we measure the real outcomes of this social creation. What matters is the spirit in and behind the state, not ideal types or specimens.

The state has always been an attempt to parcel up our home-land—based on different mythologies of what could become heavens, nirvanas, or places with water—into smaller lots, each with a title of possession for a special and unique people, each intended for those who are deemed to be most deserving. A state has traditionally been where we create history by locking ourselves into a specific pattern or way of life, so that the present and the future are no more than the repetition of an idyllic past. Now we can see the state as a place where we learn from history and test our morality, where we can change both if we find them wanting and outmoded, and where the past does not have to be a predictor of the future. The new state is always changing, always adapting, never static.

Are we on the verge of finding a solution that has, until now, remained just beyond our imagination? Will we at last have freedom and equality without empire? Can we have citizenship, and even nationality, without asserting an ideal or a quintessence of belonging? We are asking if it is desirable, or even possible, to remove the race-based concept of nation from the state and still have a civil, cultured, and morally upright people. Indeed, we ask, does making us better human beings have anything to do with race?

If we hold on to this moment of creation and develop the lessons that history and morality have for us about race, we will soon be approaching times that would have been unthinkable for those who were historically of a different view, particularly those who would have considered the elevation of this new morality a descent into hell. That we will perhaps soon see the day when race does not matter is the main claim of this book. This would be the beginning of something new, a great leap of faith into the future, and it would be marked by a new attitude. For the first time in our history, we would not be bothered enough to care about the outcome. It could be an end to a history, a moment whose arrival has been trumpeted many times before, without living up to the expected billing. This time, the arrival seems more plausible.

Already the fledging signs of this spirit of triumph can be found in the northernmost part of North America, which has traditionally been where the liberating spirit of Modernity reveals itself in its many forms. This time, Canada, with its unique population drawn from the four corners of the world, is the proving ground. Markedly, this is not the Canada imagined by either Smuts or Garvey; this is not a white man's country. Officially, and for the first time in our history, it is a nation-state without races, or at least without an official race. This time, both the structure and the blue-print of the Modern nation-state are Canadian. And so too is the new spirit to be housed in it—a spirit culled from all humanity, a spirit of different peoples united together without a race.

Theirs are the voices of a New Babel, if not a New Jerusalem, where the emphasis is on difference and diversity instead of uniform sameness. Canadians claim a lineage that is proudly impure, and the recognition that it's mixed is viewed as a strength from which Canadians claim excellence. They celebrate many different cultures and gods, and no longer try to separate them-selves into clean and unclean, godly and ungodly, chosen and damned. Idealistically, the land they occupy is still God-given, but they accept, without contradiction, that the same land has been given by other gods to other peoples, with no one having exclusive ownership and no inheritance being promised to some future generation that is supposedly marked by ethnic or racial purity.[12] They are pouring new wine into old skins without fear that the skins will burst. The god they worship has no specific image. Their land is to be shared by the many and not the few.

This is a place without ideals or idols, where the state is not immortal, where to conform is death and to be indeterminate is freedom and life. Race begins with the thought of immortality and conformity; racism begins when we put into action practices that indicate that society is permanent, that identities are known and fixed, and that human nature has reached the point where change is no longer necessary. Race is when some specimens are declared perfect and all others are judged by this exacting standard. This is a society that does not claim to be perfect but merely attempts to improve one day after another. Thou shall not take unto thyself any idols becomes the moral imperative of a raceless society that is multicultural. Thou shall not kill or hold in bondage any person— particularly not the stranger, the immigrant, or the ethnically different—becomes the ethical appeal that sustains a way of life.

This is the unity of purpose to which we now officially cling. And we cling to it in good faith, as the practitioners of multiculturalism, as an indeterminate ideal for Canada.

Indeed, at a cursory glance, Canadians are doing all the things that the men and women of old had made taboo in the quest for a patriotism and a nationalism that were strong, healthy, and durable. Most taboo of all is that old proscription that there should be a primacy of civilization, especially one that claims to be both European and Christian, or even African and Christian. Good Christians like Smuts and Garvey would have been mortified by what civilization has come to—and in Canada, of all places. Just a generation ago, multi-ethnicity and multiculturalism were only dreams. But one man's dream is often another's nightmare. Where one person sees a coming delight and a new life, another imagines only fear and death.

Such was the fear of the longest-serving prime minister of Canada, a man who said that his service to his people would have been in vain if he had overseen anything other than the preservation of a white man's country. Prime Minister William Lyon Mackenzie King was a good friend and associate of Smuts's, and the two men, intent on achieving the same goals, bound their countries in a special relationship. Their dream was shared by the president of the United States, Woodrow Wilson, a man who also aimed to save humanity from its own imagining and warlike tendencies.

With Smuts at his side at the International Peace Conference in 1919, Wilson promoted the League of Nations as the pinnacle of human achievement. With Smuts at his side at the various imperial conferences of the British Empire, King fashioned a special relationship between the Confederation of Canada and the Union of South Africa. Together, the three men hoped to maintain an international order based on dividing the world into superior and inferior groups. Wilson, we must recall, was the president who effectively reintroduced race officially into the American nation-state by instituting segregationist policies, taking people with Black skin out of the Modern nation-state. This was particularly the case when he allowed segregation to occur in federal institutions, especially the post office. In that one act, he reversed efforts by the federal government that had been ongoing since the creation of the United States, through the expansion of the Louisiana Purchase and the turmoil of the American Civil War, to champion the rights of African-Americans. In the world of Smuts, King, and Wilson, Blacks were relegated to second-class status.

These men were products of their times and their history. Fortunately, time has moved on. We can pass judgment on them, but we must do so in the knowledge that soon others will pass judgment on us. History does not end, even if, in moving on, it is always passing judgment on the past.

Today, the nightmares so feared by these three international statesmen are part of the reality of living in the Modern world. Black skin is fast losing its relevance as a means of setting limits on ambitions and citizenship. Are we approaching the day Martin Luther King, Jr., spoke of almost a half-century ago when he predicted that "the sons of former slaves and the sons of former slave owners will be able to sit down together at the table of brotherhood"? Are we at last nearing a time when boys and girls will be "judged not by the colour of their skin but by the content of their character"? Is this the reality we can now offer to young Black boys and girls not only in Montgomery, Atlanta, Buxton, and Johannesburg, but also in Toronto, Montreal, Calgary, Halifax, and Sudbury?

This book argues that we now have the opportunity to produce such times. This would allow what is euphemistically still called Western civilization to enter into a new millennium, or a new spirit of Modernity, *an era in which, for the first time in the Modern human experience, race does not matter.* In this new era, the intentions that precede the actions in any social relationship will be for a good that is raceless. If our actions follow our thoughts, this new good will be upon us, or at least we will have made our best efforts to bring it about.

The beginnings of this new era can be seen in the multicultural composition of Canada, and in the ease with which young Canadians accept the multicultural nature of their state and their citizenship. It can be seen in England, where, according to the census, more communities are becoming predominantly Black. It can be seen in South Africa, where power has shifted, with seemingly few hiccups, from white hands to Black. It can be seen in the southern United States, where a growing number of police chiefs, governors, and other elected officials are Black. And it can be seen in popular culture the world over, where it is now acceptable for a Black man to appear as God in the movies, for Black actors to carry off top awards, and for much of modern music to be drawn from Black culture.

Most of all, it can be seen in what Western civilization is coming to mean: a way of life that draws on the strengths of people from all parts of the world. Indeed, having dispensed with using race as a method for national development, we have also dropped from favour the idea of dividing humanity into separate civilizations, into worlds that are ranked from first through third. Now we know that countries once considered to be of one world can have regions within them from different and contradictory worlds. There is unity in diversity. The boundaries between our thoughts and our actions have been fused. Now we must make sure that the potential in this moment comes forth.

But for many, this lived experience was not supposed to be. (So much for purposefulness when devised by human minds!) Thankfully, the world marched to its own beat and, over time, followed its own designs. Indeed, in the long run everything turned out for the good. But at the beginning of Modernity, Blacks were intentionally excluded from the affairs of state. Their skin declared to others first their biological and then their cultural inferiority. They had no official place, no standing, no privileges in the Modern state or in international affairs. Modernity worked out of European and Christian civilizations. Its goal was to create an environment to allow the greatest in human achievements. Society, it was believed, would provide individuals with a culture that would, in due course, civilize them, turning them almost into gods, but for the fact that unlike gods they would die. The attainment of citizenship in these cultures marked the achievement of the highest levels of human perfection. Hence, citizens became the most endowed and privileged individuals. This we see in the rise of jingoism, patriotism, and nationalism. Citizenship was predicated predominantly on separation. Exclusion was based, in the main, on the colour of the skin, ethnicity, or culture. The nation-state was the finishing school for the elites of humanity, those who would become citizens of a white and European-style nation-state. Looking back, we can now claim with a morality borne out by history that such attempts to exclude specific groups from the nation-state were evil and should not be continued in the present or carried forward into the future.

Black-skinned people were considered to be less than human, or at least less fully realized than those perfected beings of the higher-achieving civilizations, cultures, and nation-states. They were held as chattel slaves and then in apprenticeship and tutelage until the white elites of the world deemed them civilized enough to govern themselves. Theirs was a culture marked by permanent alienation, a culture where the lived experience was always lagging behind the perfection attained when humans reach their full potential. And those who argued against Modernity's dominant model were often themselves ostracized and excluded from society.

Other non-European groups, according to the dominant Western view, would naturally make their own attempts at state formation. But because they were perceived as inferior in thoughts and actions to Europeans, they would, naturally, apply inferior structures and methods, have inferior goals, and experience poor-quality results. Europeans would produce the gem of a superior Western civilization. This was the natural order of the world, the foundation on which long-lasting social and ethical relations would be based. At the heart of this thinking was always *race*, which was so much more than the colour of the skin, the shape of nose, the curl of the hair, or the fullness of the lips. Even when physically free, Blacks and other visible and racialized minorities were to be excluded from the prototypical state and from involvement in all the Modern institutions and agencies. This was the thinking behind segregation in the United States, apartheid in South Africa, reservations and ethnic homelands in Canada, and the expulsions of criminals and the mentally and physically disabled from states around the world.

But today, those who were once excluded are taking up leading roles in institutions, agencies, and states that were once intended exclusively for a different people. This is not to suggest that there is no longer any racism, or that there is an equitable distribution of Blacks and other minorities within national institutions or in business. But the attitude towards Blacks and other minorities and their place in society has changed. As long as the intentions remain good, positive actions will follow, even if slowly. The journey is incremental: a slow forward pass rather than a quick dash to the finish line. What's important is that there is no official turning back to reclaim and reconstitute ideals that are now discredited. New social relationships are becoming set and, in many cases, have been fully accepted by the elites of society. The ideological turn has already happened, and that is the hardest part to achieve. We must feed the spirit of a new time and seize its goodness.

In the current social climate, there are a few cases where racial discrimination and profiling are still viewed as ethically acceptable, although it is usually for those who are not considered part of the nation-state. We see this, for example, with the racial profiling the United States has engaged in to combat terrorism, when individuals who show up at airports are required to prove their citizenship and automatic right of (re)entry. Why is racism practised in the breach rather than as the norm? And does this mean that the Modern state has been built on a shifting foundation?

It has not been easy to overcome racism in Canada or internationally. And the debates over racial profiling, Black youth gangs, and the place in the social hierarchy of immigrants from predominantly Black countries prove that in some areas the struggle still continues. There is an ocular deficit that is emblematic of the alienation that still exists in Canada. In other words, what we see—in terms of the numbers of visible minorities in various government institutions and agencies and in business in general—is very different from what the ideal would suggest. It is the difference between the dream of full citizenship and the current realities of the difficulty attaining it. The deficit can be a measurement of hope or of despair, of what is achievable but is viewed as very unlikely. It is a deficit that, we hope, gets smaller every day.

The unreconciled visions of Canada, where the theory promises one thing and the lived reality is very different, are generational. One look at the top echelons of government and business reveals them still to be disproportionately white. But it also reveals that our leaders are aging. Soon, they will need to be replaced, and then Canada will have a chance to reconcile theory and practice by filling the vacated positions according to new rules and regulations. The future seems to point towards a world in which Black skin colour will have no bearing on how we see ourselves constitutively, as nations or citizens. In the absence of full sight and knowledge, we operate in the spirit of hope.

But do these developments mean that Blackness now has no real social or ethical purpose? Do they mean that we are marching inevitably towards a new Modernity? This book, while arguing against complacency, strongly suggests that as a point of pride, there should always be meaning to having Black skin. This meaning has always been a hidden element of Modernity, and it is caught in much of the mythology of Western civilization—including the mythology captured in the dreams of Martin Luther King, Jr., and others like him. Black skin is a mark from the gods, a reminder that we are all human and that none of us, Black or white, should ever forget our humanity. We must not forget how easy it is for some groups of people to declare themselves morally and ethically superior. We must not forget how easy it is to find reasons to enslave others, whether physically or mentally.

People with Black skin must stand as a reminder that we are all the sons and daughters of slaves, and that none of us is a descendant of gods. They will continue to carry this responsibility—which some may call a burden, but I view as an issue of pride and self-consciousness—into the future. We are all human. On this score, the body never lies. Like the state, it always dies. And we see the face of humanity in all the places and positions of the world, even in locations where some were not supposed to be but have claimed triumphantly. They have defeated race by lifting up hope and faith.

FROM THE EARLIEST TIMES, humans have tried to release the two sides of the social and political cords representing diametrically opposite ways of state formation. On one side of this binary, there is the attempt to produce unity out of the diversity and difference that make up humanity itself. This is what we usually mean by ethnicity, and we associate it with progress, advancement, and even Modernism. On this side of civilization, all the distinct groups that make up the universal that is humanity have advancement, progress, and Modernism as their goals. The pride they take in their identity and culture is grounded in their presumed differences.

But there is always the other side, and that is race, the way we tend often to think of others. We admire those whom we consider to be equal or superior to us. Disdain is reserved for those who are less than us, our inferiors. This is race, a quality that transcends ethnicity, especially when it is a label of natural inferiority. Race is something that we confer on others, and often at their displeasure. Race is a bogus determinant, however, if only because these days few people give themselves a race. People do not, generally, inflict abuse and violence on themselves; to do so would be a kind of social suicide. Instead of negatively labelling ourselves, therefore, we do it to other people, especially those we feel most deserving, or those who cannot stop us. Race is usually about the Other, and about weakness and the violence we can inflict on others. It is seldom a mark of authority or self-ownership.

In the past five hundred years, the nation-state has tried to bind together these two cords. But perhaps it is not wise to attempt to untangle such ends, even if each supposedly offers a path to human happiness. Perhaps it is better to make a bold strike and let the pieces fall as they may. That way, the end result will be unplanned, unscripted, and novel. Gone will be the malice of forethought, the burden of having made moral decisions and then put them into action. The gamble might pay off as the beginning of a time when race does not matter. This is the new spirit of Modernity.

The moment seems to be almost upon us when we will be able to live as if there were no single and distinct purpose to human activity, when we will be able to act as if there were no specific single outcome to our efforts. Indeed, it might soon be possible to assume that the world has its own purpose, a purpose free of the desires and wishes of any particular group. This might be the pivotal moment that is sometimes called the end of history. Some, like the writer and political scientist Francis Fukuyama, saw the end of history come with the fall of the Berlin Wall, that barrier that separated the Modern world into eastern and western camps. (Although these camps were supposedly both democratic—either socially, as in the east, or economically, as in the west.) This was purportedly when the spirit of freedom—the same spirit that had driven history for at least two millenniums—had come fully into its own. It had taken a specific form—one that was both eastern and western, old and new, universal and particular. Spirit had finally taken a course, and it supposedly chose capitalism and globalism as its most perfect forms.

However, as Fukuyama noted in his book *The End of History or the Last Man,* in making its choice spirit seemed merely to be validating something that was preordained. In Fukuyama's analysis, spirit is in the end predetermined, whether it chooses the path of capitalism or the approach dreamed of by Smuts or Garvey. But those holding this view are trapped in the thinking that there is a single purpose to life; they don't view life as offering a dynamism that is purposeless, often random, and always incapable of being harnessed by any one group of people.

According to Fukuyama, the end of history brought with it the triumph of a certain brand of democracy and freedom. The last man is the ultimate perfect human specimen, a cultural capitalist so evolved that she or he could function fully in the freedoms of a liberal democracy. This spirit was made manifest in the United States, among capitalist ideals originally founded on Christian ethics. The American melting pot is the archetype.

On reflection, Fukuyama might have been a bit hasty in his declaration. The struggle for full freedom that has marked Modernity continues on several fronts and takes many different forms. The keenest of these is still race, for even in the United States of America, home to the spirit of freedom of which Fukuyama wrote, race remains a major feature of the national body politic. It still stirs emotions and sparks resentment. There are wounds that have not yet healed and still run as deep as in the days of transatlantic slavery, when they were inflicted. They are there every time a Confederate flag flutters in the breeze over a southern monument or state capital. It seems the much-vaunted melting pot has proven inconsistent at taking imperfect specimens from around the world and returning them transfigured as the pure alloys of America.

Yet another end of history was supposed to have occurred some time ago. "'It is no use,' said an eminent Colonial Office secretary to myself when I once remonstrated, 'to speak about it any longer. The thing is done. The great colonies are gone. It is but a question of a year or two.'"[13] So wrote James Anthony Froude, recounting his conversation with a colonial officer, in his book *Oceana: Or, England and Her Colonies*. The book was published in 1886, in a moment that, in Froude's opinion, was supposed to mark the beginning of the end of history for the British Empire. The commonwealth that was supposedly the successor to Alexander the Great's Roman Empire was crumbling into many nations and states. No longer could it be seen as a federation of different peoples and cultures around the world. Unity was shattering. The centre could no longer hold the whole together.

Froude was one of the foremost authorities on English history and culture in Britain. He was very well connected in British society—an intimate friend of Thomas Carlyle, the rabid anti-Black and anti-Irish philosopher; a confidant of at least two British prime ministers, Benjamin Disraeli and William Gladstone; and a companion to several members of the British Cabinet. Froude was also an eminent scholar, having reached the honoured position of Regius professor of modern history at Oxford, and he drew his references for the unfurling of cultures and civilizations from the Greek tragedies (describing British rule, for example, as the modern-day equivalent of Odysseus's bow, which could be used only by its rightful owner, the one favoured by the gods).

His book *The English in the West Indies: Or, The Bow of Ulysses* came to be associated with the term "white man's burden," a phrase used to describe the supposed responsibility Europeans had to civilize Africans, no matter where in the world they were living.

Among his major works was the twelve-volume *History of England,* an influential study of English culture and civilization around the globe, and especially in the British Empire. In addition, Froude had been the editor of *Fraser's Magazine,* considered one of the most progressive organs of Victorian thought, and a publication whose format was copied throughout the British Empire. (In Canada, *Saturday Night* magazine was patterned on it.) Froude's thinking would inform many of the attitudes about race in our times.

What was about to end in the 1880s, in Froude's mind, was something special. He wrote, "Those were the days of progress by leaps and bounds, of 'unexampled prosperity,' of the apparently boundless future which the repeal of the Corn Laws had opened upon British industry and trade. The fate of Great Britain was that it was to become the world's great workshop. Her people were to be kept at home and multiply. With cheap labour and cheap coal we could defy competition, and golden streams would flow down in ever-gathering volumes over landowners and millowners and shipowners.... The 'hands' and the 'hands'' wives and children? Oh yes, they too would do very well: wages would rise, food would be cheap, employment constant. The colonies brought us nothing. The empire brought us nothing, save expense for armaments and possibilities of foreign complications. Shorn of these wild shoots we should be like an orchard tree pruned of its luxuriance, on which the fruit would grow richer and more abundant."[14] Here, too, Froude was positing a singular purpose to life, one that would triumph over all pretenders in the end.

What Froude was lamenting was the death of the British Empire—a death that would appear more certain in the first decades of the twentieth century. Unlike no other before it, this empire was built solidly on race. But what race had built, it was suddenly in the process of dismantling, a process that was most obvious in the colonies, where the generic race question became the more specific Irish question, Indian question, South African question, French question (in Canada), and the overall question of the colonies—all of which revolved around race in some fashion.

Speaking to a group of philosophers in Edinburgh, Froude lamented how the world order that had long sustained the British Empire was unravelling according to a time and spirit of its own. "I decided after some reflection that for once I would leave the history of the past and turn to a question of present interest and the present time," Froude said to the members of the Philosophical Institute. His 1880 lecture was one of the earliest condemnations of what we now call pre-emptive strikes, when we act militarily out of mere suspicion and because of a fear of the stranger. Froude described the effect that that kind of attitude was having in South Africa: "For the South African question is a very knotty one indeed, and the knots can only be untied when the British people will please to pay attention to it. We can hardly say that it is of no importance to us. We have been killing about twenty thousand people in South Africa—people who had done us no harm; we only feared that perhaps they might do us harm. We have annexed a country as large as France, which belonged to Dutchmen. Dutchmen do not like to have their independence taken away from them any more than we do, and nobody exactly knows why we did it."[15]

For Froude, the race question was, in essence, about superiors and inferiors, the learned and the unlearned, and a civil order where everyone knew her or his unchanging place. "There is no success possible to any man save in finding and obeying those who are his superiors," he wrote in *Oceana,* where he was probably thinking of both a ship at sea and the ship of state. "But to follow mock superior, and to be cheated in the process! Who could wish that we would submit to that? If captains and officers were discovered to have never learnt their business, to be doing nothing but amuse themselves and consume the ship's stores, the crew would have to depose them and do the best they could with their own understandings; but if the crew were persons of sense, they would probably look out at their best speed for other officers, and trust to their own lights for as short a time as possible."[16]

While Froude was in fact describing his journey from England to the Cape of Good Hope on a ship called the *Australasian,* no doubt his mind was on another vessel—the ship of state made so famous by the philosopher and anti-democrat Plato. The latter was a ship that had no order, where crew and passengers had mistaken notions of their own importance, social standing, virtues, and abilities. Even though they were inferior by nature to the captains, the deckhands believed they could actually pilot the ship to a safe harbour. Instead, they disrupted the voyage with their attempts to impose a new order. In the end, they wrecked the ship, all because those who were naturally inferior would not respect the differences with which nature endowed different groups of people. None of the deckhands wanted to be positioned based on his virtues or natural talents. And all were likely to wreck the ship on the rocks, in exactly the scenario that Froude felt had already come to the ship of state that was Britain and the colonies.

For Froude, the evidence of the shipwreck was clear. Squalor is the unavoidable result when humans put the emphasis on political economy rather than the social need for a common good. Froude promoted instead the civilizing efforts of striving for the highest good of a specific people, nation, or race. This was a humanism that aimed to produce the highest evolved citizens. They would be made and perfected within a nation-state that was governed by rational laws, a society as perfect as if a superior race of people or gods had made it. Within such a society, they would be able to achieve the highest levels of intellectual and human attainment, and it would all be done in civility and according to rational rules. However, this state would have strata of types of individuals arrayed in an order ranging from superior to inferior. The stratification was supposedly based on race—with racialized groups of people finding the standing that is most natural for them within the hierarchy.

As long as the ship was not taken over and an unnatural order imposed—with inferior members thinking too highly of themselves; with everyone trying to be captain; or with the passengers and crew becoming drunk from overindulging on their own self-worth—it would sail safely into its intended harbour, arriving on time, no matter the storms it encountered on the way. But to accept a social order based on natural attributes would be anathema to those in the state who were desirous of change—those whose behaviour and thinking were "unnatural"; those who would run the ship of state aground. As Froude exclaimed, "It seems now that this era too is closed; science has come back upon us, and democracy along with her. What next?"[17] Indeed, he wondered, what further tragedies would come now that people were relying on science and democracy to destroy the old order, in which a minority of superiors was no longer expected to rule a majority of inferiors and science could be used to blunt what he thought were clearly the social intentions of nature.

Yet while change is all around us, there is so much that never changes. Froude observed: "Those stars on which we were gazing from the deck of the 'Australasian,' those seas through which we were rushing, age after age had looked on them and seen them as we saw them. How many mariners, each once at the front of the world's history, had sailed over those same waters! Phoenicians, Carthaginians, Greeks, Romans, Norsemen, Crusaders, Italians, Spaniards, Portuguese, French, English, all in their turn. To each of these it had seemed once to belong, and they steered their courses by the same stars which are now shining on ourselves. Knights and warriors, pirates and traders, great admirals, discoverers of new continents, of whose names history is full—Columbus and Santa Cruz, Drake and Grenville, Rodney and Nelson—had passed where we were passing, between the Azores and the Canaries; all burning with fires of hope and purpose which have long since sunk to ashes."[18]

For Froude, one of the unchangeables humanity had discovered was the British system of developing separate civil societies for the superior and inferior races, represented, respectively, by the British and Blacks (as epitomized by Africans around the world). The ideal government, according to Froude and others of like mind, was represented by the mother-and-daughter relationship between Britain and her colonies, and the oldest and most accomplished example of this relationship existed between England and Canada, a white man's country.

The poorest form of government, Froude claimed, was that practised by free Blacks in Haiti, where, he said, people lived in the worst human squalor. Like Plato's ship of fools—where all the untrained and uncivil drunks were trying to become captain and violence was a way of life—this ship of state had ceased progressing on a steady course towards its harbour and instead was going backwards, or even sinking under the weight of its own filth. This was so unlike, Froude thought, neighbouring Jamaica, then still firmly under the guidance and control of the English. In that island state, where Marcus Garvey would be born and nurtured, the ruling elites had, in Froude's eyes, been enlightened enough to opt for a return to crown colony rule in 1865, rejecting the greater levels of political freedom that would have come with Black majority rule for the absolute of white minority rule.

This choice was the very opposite of the dreams and aspirations of the revolution that had produced an independent Haiti. At a time when white colonies like Canada, New Zealand, Australia, and Newfoundland were demanding greater measures of self-rule from Britain, the Jamaican elites had decided on a "backwards" move, putting themselves totally under British governance. This came on the eve of Canadian Confederation, as the country moved towards greater responsibilities in government and, ultimately, to full independence as a sovereign nation-state. In Froude's opinion, the Jamaican elites were choosing the wisest and most natural course, the one that would avoid the chaos and degeneracy that he saw resulting inevitably from rule by Blacks. Jamaica was safeguarding its future progress by not even attempting to follow the Canadian model, which would lead ultimately to dominion status within the British Empire. But at the same time it was not accepting the dangers and uncertainties of the Haitian model of development.

Froude became even more definite in his views when he sailed for Haiti to have confirmed what he had long suspected and to see first-hand the instability caused by the power struggles of people he considered racially too inferior even to govern themselves. But in looking at the human misery of Haiti, he overlooked one important thing: how much of it was caused not by the Haitians themselves but by those who thought they were agents of history. What Froude failed to recognize was the handiwork of those who intended to prove, as he and others believed, that Black-skinned people were not fit to rule themselves. (This, too, was the lesson in Jamaica's return to crown colony status—in effect, white rule—at the behest of a white elite that felt threatened and encircled by increasing demands for Black rule.) And they did prove it—by ensuring that Haiti remained an economic basket case. It was to be the dystopia for the world's utopia that was a white man's country. This, unhappily, is one of the legacies of the attempts to manufacture and shape a specific history.

Froude was establishing himself as the intellectual forebear of Smuts and others like him. He sought to ensure, wherever humanly possible, that South Africa became a white man's jewel in the crown of the British Empire, a colony as respected as its bigger sister, Canada. Most important, he sought to ensure that it did not become an African version of Haiti. For Froude, Haiti had unwittingly regressed to a point before the start of time, rather than progressing naturally towards the end of time. Canada and South Africa were the ideal ways to expand a lifespan that he called Western or Christian civilization. They were an ideal to which other nations could never aspire.

This was a sentiment captured in a song so often chanted at harbours as non-whites descended from immigrant ships in the early part of the twentieth century. Claiming to be fighting for God, the king, and a white man's country, onlookers sang, "This is the voice of the West and it speaks to the world. Our watchword be 'God save the King.' White Canada for ever. We welcome as brothers all white men. But the shifty yellow race whose word is vain … must find another place."[19] For Froude, it was natural for whites to sing songs like this in South Africa, Canada, Australia, New Zealand, the southern United States, and anywhere else where whites lived apart from or ruled Blacks, imposing a social order that ensured the two races never mixed.

AT THIS POINT IN TIME, we can pass judgment on the success Froude and others like him had in exporting the Canadian model of a nation-state. This new spirit results in a new approach to a problem that has always confounded humanity: How possible is it to become truly human either as an individual or as part of a group? Resolving the kinks in the Canadian prototype became as important a factor in developing a new world order as Alexander the Great's cutting the Gordian knot at the beginning of Modern times. For like the multi-headed hydra that it is, race simply transformed itself into different problems and challenges, donning new disguises to keep up with the changing times. Alexander the Great went on to create a mighty empire, one of the first successful attempts at globalization. He wanted people from different lands and cultures to be bound together in one nationality and as one citizenry. They would be held together by the glue of rational laws, like the forces for good and for advancement that were supposed to radiate out of Rome. Everyone coming under its influence would be part of a human family of equals. Even Saul, the Christian apostle later renamed Paul, invoked his Roman citizenship to avoid the more demeaning treatment given to non-Roman citizens in his day. Paul was the prototype of the ideal multicultural citizen. His hyphenated identities were put on or taken off as he wished, each one used to earn him the maximum protection available.

Idealistically, the difference would be between those who were recognized in the British Empire as belonging under its wings and those who were not so blessed. But the Gordian knot gave way to a series of smaller entanglements, each one spawned by the awakening of national fervour among the peoples who were to have come together as one in the new arrangement. The social theorist Hannah Arendt argues that the British Empire, like all empires of this type, offered nothing that could have prevented the natives, or other subjected peoples, from developing national consciousness and clamouring for sovereignty and independence—though its efforts might have retarded the process somewhat.[20] It was during this period of change and transformation that Canada, a young country coming into adulthood as a Modern nation-state, emerged as a leading actor in the development of a new international order.

As most everyone remembers, the then prime minister, caught up in the spirit of those times, had prophesied that the twentieth century would belong to Canada. According to Wilfrid Laurier, Canada would claim the century by taking over the leading role in the British Empire and saving it from total collapse. The danger to the empire, in Laurier's view, was that the British government had become confused, for it was torn between the competing ideals of good government and equality for all subjects, Black or white. As Froude once asked, What next—democracy? Equality of this kind, according to many of the empire's white intelligentsia, was unnatural and contradictory to the ideals of good government. Inferior people had to be ruled, often with a firm hand, for the natural good of humanity. The Canadian elites, the argument went, as the pioneers of responsible government within the British Empire, understood natural law and had perfected its practice. Because of this, they could look forward to at least a century of success. The elites in England, meanwhile, could only lament that the good life was all over. Prime Minister Laurier was on the same page as Froude when he made his prediction about the inevitable triumph of race planning. Without it, he said, we'd witness the untimely death of the greatest civilization then developed and known. The best representative of this superior model was the Canadian dominion—the place where the prototype of so-called responsible government was field tested.

Laurier's views on race were not unique. All over the United States, Britain, France, Brazil, and the Caribbean (particularly in Haiti, Jamaica, and the British territories), people debated the future of the Black race, the perils of Black rule and sovereignty, and the perceived dangers of mixing Blacks and whites. Laurier was on good terms with the men then crafting a racist state in South Africa, including Louis Botha, the prime minister, and his constitutional minister, Jan Smuts. The relationship, according to Brian Douglas Tennyson in his book *Canadian Relations with South Africa,* was "based on similar attitudes and objectives in the imperial framework, an awareness of their uniqueness as the only self-governing colonies not overwhelmingly British in population, and the personal rapport which developed between Laurier and Botha."[21] It would continue with Robert Borden, Mackenzie King, and subsequent Canadian leaders. In fact, in 1947 King formulated the immigration policy that was intended to make Canada a white country. Officially codifying what had been the practice for a long time, the policy depended on the use of the passport to regulate and keep out Blacks and other non-whites and non-Europeans. At the same time, South Africa was using the passbook to create a white republic under apartheid.

Laurier's special relationship with South Africa would remain strong and personal when Smuts succeeded Botha.

Laurier openly advised those behind the South African Union on dealing with their race question. Brian Douglas Tennyson contends that Laurier took great interest in what was happening in South Africa after the Boer War because of parallels he saw in Canada, and because of the new role he wanted Canada to play in the British Empire. "It is not surprising either," Tennyson claims, "that South African political leaders, as they worked their way towards a union of their four colonies, looked to Canada as the only bicultural Dominion in the Empire for guidance."

Laurier also had a practical reason for encouraging the South Africans to forge a united, self-governing dominion. He believed that South Africa would be dominated by Afrikaners, whom he felt were more likely to support Canada's positions against the English at future colonial conferences. Already England and its white dominions, led by Canada, were feuding over the racial treatment of non-whites in the empire. England was arguing that they should be treated with greater equality, while Canada and South Africa favoured a second-class status.

It was as an adviser to Botha's constitutional minister and eventual successor, Smuts, that Laurier had his biggest impact on South Africa's constitution. He advised Smuts, for example, to ensure that South Africa had a strong, centralized federation with some powers delegated to the provinces. "South Africans like Botha and Smuts looked to Canada as the only relatively happy example of a bicultural state," Tennyson argues. He asserts that Rodolphe Lemieux, the Canadian representative at the inauguration of the South African Parliament in 1910, told Laurier, "Canada is looked upon as the *elder brother*. We are supposed to *lead* in everything. There is a general feeling that as a Dominion, we have been a decided success and that in order to be a success South Africa should be following in our footsteps."[22] In fact, in arguing for responsible government for South Africa, Smuts had cited the Canadian precedent of 1906. Later, according to Tennyson, Smuts told a Canadian audience "that 'if we have reached a happy solution of our great racial [*sic*] question in South Africa, it is largely due to the precedent that you have set.' Asked if Canada's influence has been 'a real one' in the evolution of South African self-government, Smuts later told Mackenzie King that Laurier had been 'very helpful. His letters to Botha were important.'"[23]

There is overwhelming evidence in Smuts's private papers of how this special relationship developed. In exchanges with leading South African constitutional officials, there is ample discussion of Canada and the need for South Africa to follow its lead. The premier of the Cape Colony, J. X. Merriman, wrote Smuts, "I hope you have been able to read that book about Canada that I mentioned, *The Race Question in Canada* by [André] Siegfried.[24] I sent a copy to [South Africa's minister of justice, Colin Fraser] Steyn which I am sure he would lend you. It is of surpassing interest to us here. But if we can ever work together we ought to send the best men we can to study—Australia, Canada, and Switzerland—from our point of view as affecting us."[25] Smuts in turn wrote Merriman, "The Canadian Constitution supplies some very useful ideas for us in South Africa."[26]

At this time, discussions of the future of South Africa were taking place within a specific framework that was based on a hierarchy of races. The mood of these times was captured by Lord Selborne, then the South African governor and a man who was in constant contact with Lord Grey, his Canadian counterpart. (Before coming to Canada, Lord Grey had been a director of the South African Company.) Lord Selborne wrote to Smuts to relay his view on race relations—views he'd probably also channelled to Lord Grey and to Laurier.

"The Black man," he wrote, "is absolutely incapable of rivalling the white man. If the white man is ever out-rivalled by the Black man, it will be entirely the fault of the white man. No one can have any experience of the two races without feeling the intrinsic superiority of the white man. All history in addition proves it." Lord Selborne said that in the United States, the Black man had been under the influence of civilization for at least three times as long as he had in South Africa. In the U.S., he said, there were no legal impediments to his evolution, and Blacks had been given the same educational and economic opportunities as whites. Yet Blacks were unable to compete. Once again, there appeared to be an unwillingness to understand why the described conditions should exist. Lord Selborne neglected to mention that Blacks in America had been subjected to direct and persistent inhumane treatment. Without this mention, what was produced could be cited as incontrovertible proof of an inferior race and culture.

Indeed, Selborne said, whites in South Africa need not fear Blacks. "A black man may emerge, from time to time, like Booker Washington in the United States of America or Khama in South Africa, who is centuries ahead of his fellow black men; but these exceptions only prove the rule, and it is my profound belief that the white man has nothing to fear from giving the black man the freest opportunities to evolve himself under the best conditions and free from any artificial impediment."[27]

It is worth pointing out that Lord Selborne's was a moderate view in the South African constitutional debate. His belief was that whites should not leave the natives without hope by stripping them of their basic humanity and denying them all political recognition, including the vote. Similar views were being echoed in Canada at the same time, and indeed they resurfaced again much later, when the country began to grapple with its own Native questions.

Eventually, a stream of official and unofficial visitors did flow between Canada and South Africa, providing a steady exchange of information. A book of speeches published annually by the Empire Club bears record to the exchanges—and to the spirit of the times in which they were undertaken.[28] For example, in a speech to the club in 1909, Sir J. Percy Fitzpatrick, a member of the legislative assembly of Pretoria, Transvaal, celebrated the Canadian contribution to South Africa. He said, "It is quite impossible for a South African to rise before a Canadian audience without first speaking for South Africa in acknowledgment and gratitude for the help that you gave us, not only in the War when you sent of your kith and kin, but in the subsequent period of the reconstruction. Many of your men died there, but they are not lost to you or to us. You can believe me that they are more eloquent preachers of a great doctrine than any of us who live can be. In the reconstruction we had the benefit and help from your men of a high example and, coming from South Africa, I would like to tell you that there is no part of the whole world whose reputation stands higher than that of Canada, as made by Canadians in South Africa."

In 1924 A. H. Tatlow, the publicity manager for the South African Rail Ways and Harbours in Johannesburg, told a meeting of the same club that Canada should cement the bonds between the two countries with increased trade. That goal, he said, was partly the reason he and his delegation were touring the country. "We feel that if we could only persuade you people of the North to come and see us in the South the result would be good for both; that we would understand each other better; trade relations would gradually become established and improved, and all these things would make for mutual benefit."

As late as 1956, when public opinion in Canada and internationally was beginning to move against South Africa, some Canadian elites were still singing the praises of that country to their home audiences. One such person was Dr. George P. Gilmour, the president of McMaster University in Hamilton, Ontario, who reported to the Empire Club on a recent trip he made there. His speech was intended to evoke sympathy and understanding for South Africa, and he highlighted what he saw as parallels between

Canada and the embattled country. "Africa as a whole," the intellectual and academic reported, "has never known permanent European settlement until relatively recent times. Nor has it ever had a high civilization of its own nor a democratic tradition in society. Yet in the Union of South Africa all three of those things are being attempted." He went on to say:

> Men are determined to make it a white man's country, the permanent home of people whose homelands were in Europe. They are attempting to introduce a high civilization, to bring Western industrial methods in mining, in agriculture and in manufacturing. They are hopeful of bringing a democratic tradition to bear in a territory where history does not encourage that experiment and where many "Europeans" do not think of democracy in our sense of responsible government. If we feel that South Africans are not doing as well as we think we are doing, we must remember that their continent has the three-fold disadvantage I have mentioned.

> Surrounding and interpenetrating the land occupied by these two and three-quarter million Europeans are eight and three-quarter million "natives," who are Bantu (not Negroes but Bantu) and aboriginals. Such figures are meaningless to us until we put them into terms of our own situation. If in Canada our fifteen million white population was surrounded by sixty million North American Indians who were encroaching on this campus, squatting at the back of your farm or cottage, creeping in here and there because they had no place else to go, we would know what the problem is. If in the United States there were six hundred million Negroes, people of African descent, in proportion to one hundred and fifty million white people, we would feel the problem keenly. These eight and three-quarter million natives are mostly of

Bantu blood and language. I shall not have time to speak about their settlement and their reserves, but in all fairness it should be known that these tribes were not there when white settlement began. The Bantu is almost as much a recent immigrant as is the European.

In Dr. Gilmour's eyes, Canada and South Africa shared five common problems. First, both countries struggled with two races "at war in one bosom"—the British and the Afrikaners in South Africa and the French and the English in Canada. Second, they had to contend with the poor treatment of local aboriginals by immigrant whites. Third, they had a pressing need for the right type of immigrants—that is, whites. Fourth, they faced school and work problems stemming from the "evangelizing" of the "Negro" and the "red Indian" in North America and the "natives" in South Africa. And finally, they were beset by fractious party politics.

But South Africa had one problem that Canada did not—or rather, it was a problem that Canada had long taken care of, violently and permanently. "Let us remember, when from North America we look with disapproval on the treatment of natives in South Africa, that we in Canada solved our aboriginal problem largely by never having one," Dr. Gilmour asserted. He went on to say, "The Spaniards did the dirty work centuries ago and the story of the slaughter of Indians in the Americas is no less a grim one because it happened long ago.... No wonder the South African dislikes us for pointing at him now. He may be seventeenth-century man trying to live in the twentieth century, but at least he is like we were then. As for the African population of this continent, it is only within the last few years that the United States has begun successfully to handle the problem of segregation, and the matter of schools in the United States is still far from settled. If South Africa is half a century behind, who shall blame her? And who will say that we, in the same position, would, except for a minority of enlightened spirits, do much better." Dr. Gilmour maintained that to criticize South Africa for taking care of the same problem, and in a more humane fashion than Canada and the United States had done, was morally and ethically the height of hypocrisy.

As Wilfrid Laurier would have known, the race issue was pivotal in the United States. Coming out of the Reconstruction period, President Andrew Johnson had abandoned the notion of incorporating former slaves fully into society, bowing to the pressure of the still angry Southern states after their Civil War defeat. Meanwhile, in some circles concern was growing that the presence of Blacks in government was leading to a destruction of European culture, and that Blacks were best held, for their own good, in positions of servitude. Giving in to demands from the defeated southern states, the American government rolled back the liberal and democratic rights of Blacks and introduced segregation and other Jim Crow laws to keep Blacks in their place and out of power.

But the forces of democracy and liberalism were pressing on, with debate in the American Black community centring on whether Blacks had a future in the United States or should move elsewhere. Black intellectuals like W. E. B. Du Bois[29] and Marcus Garvey[30] took different positions. Du Bois wanted full integration, whereas Garvey was advocating a "Back to Africa" relocation, a mass migration that would virtually rid the Americas of the physical presence of Blackness.

This was not a new idea. Canada had expelled Black Loyalists and Maroons in the late eighteenth century, and even Abraham Lincoln had suggested that migration might be the solution to the Black question, and that Haiti was a natural Black homeland.[31] This view was popular throughout the Americas, with the Haitian government looking favourably on the idea from time to time. As the historian H. P. Davis wrote, "Co-operating with certain prominent abolitionists of New England, [President Fabre] Geffrard made elaborate plans to bring to Haiti 'industrious men of African descent.' Some few such emigrants actually arrived, but the plan failed, owing partly to lack of proper preparation to receive and care for these people, but more because of the absence of any public interest either in Haiti or in the United States."[32]

Race was an issue all over the world, at least according to men like Froude. In his eyes, integration in the American South was not working. Britain had, among others, its Indian, Irish, and South African problems, and even in the Caribbean there were race problems. Froude had visited there and found that the region was a disaster for all, white and Black, primarily because of the mixing of races. The Caribbean British colonies were themselves acknowledging that the system under which they operated was not functioning, and for the white elites the obvious solution was to join in a federation with Canada. They feared it was just a matter of time before an expansionary United States swallowed up their islands, while Brazil would swallow up Guyana and Belize, the English outposts in Latin and Central America. The Americas would in effect be divided into three distinct areas: Brazil and its colonies; the United States of America, with the Caribbean islands as appendages; and Canada. Of these, the first two would become Black republics, while Canada would remain the sole white homeland, a nation strongly oligarchic in rule and status. To men like Laurier, Canada's problems with its French minority were inconsequential compared with those of other places. As the South African elites noticed, Canada's aboriginal questions had been neatly tucked out of sight on Native reserves or in independent homelands.

A century after Laurier made his famous prediction, we can say that he was wrong in many ways. Indeed, some would argue that the policies he espoused would have led Canada to the precipice in half a century. Failure eventually came when the country had to abandon the morality that would have been needed for it to dominate the century. Indeed, the second half of the twentieth century actually saw the country retreating from its claim to greatness, a retrenchment that placed it on the path to the land of Babel, with its many voices, languages, peoples, and cultures, instead of turning it into an Augustinian city of purity and a refuge for the chosen few.

But in many ways that Laurier would not have anticipated, Canada did fulfil the prime minister's prediction. It has become a beacon of peace, a city on the hill, and this is why the new spirit of Modernity has a home here. Although Canada was never intended to be a site for this struggle—that option was rejected at the very beginning of what we now call Canada—few things ever turn out exactly as they are imagined. And another lesson is that even when they do, there's often a disconnect between the imagined and realized, between the dream and the lived experience. Gremlins do come out of the woodwork. Imperfections are part of being human. Mind and hands, like body and soul, are not always in agreement. And while it might be possible to place matter in motion, it is not always possible to guide the motion to a chosen end. Such is the reality of the human condition.

This is why the search for well-being for all is as everlasting and as elusive as truth. Yet another lesson is that sometimes it is necessary to return to the beginning and, even if it means swallowing pride and acknowledging mistakes, choose an option that was once rejected. For the stone that the builders initially reject might be the best choice for a cornerstone. It might simply have been misrecognized, or perhaps the workmen might not have fully appreciated the quality of the materials offered them. They might have had to redo their blueprints, settling for materials that are less than ideal but are all that's available. These are the lessons of history.

The new spirit that is promised from the release of this bind looks very similar to what we have seen in history. It is the promise of racial egalitarianism and fraternity of the Haitian Revolution, now considered one of the birthdates of Modernity, the times in which we now live. The aim of the Haitian Revolution was the creation of a Black state—or more precisely, a state that was not white and would not become, through a policy of assimilation, a white man's country. In the eyes of Froude and others like him, Haiti was the bogeyman and its fate was exactly what white-only states in the Americas and elsewhere should fear. This was the same fear that paralyzed constitutional developments in South Africa, ultimately leading to apartheid and official racial separation, policies that appeared out of the very contradictions of history that eventually led to Canada's becoming an officially multicultural country.

That these developments are happening in Canada at this very moment is testimony to the resilience of the spirit of Modernity, its ability to adapt, and its power to make individuals its instruments. That Canada is still evolving as a multicultural state is perhaps the surest sign that contradictions in history are seldom fully resolved, and that often they only succeed in creating new contradictions. Every era produces problems and contradictions that have their genesis in the problems and contradictions of earlier eras, yet each contradiction takes a form and appearance that makes it quintessentially of its own time.

We can trace a lineage for multiculturalism, taking it back through the various manifestations of the struggle for freedom—apartheid, Black homelands, the reservation system, and even a primitive fear of the stranger—and showing how race was always a major determinant. In Canada today, everyone is now technically a stranger. The future is in the hands of foreigners who must become citizens and produce the babies needed for the Canada of tomorrow. The burden of preserving a nation-state into the future will in this way be detached from the old belief that there is a primordial bond between citizens and their homeland. Ethnicity and perhaps even race will be erased.

Canada will become a collection of diasporas, home to all the peoples of the world. In Canada, the ideal is that there are no social ideals.

But as usual with this spirit, there is a contradiction, and even a caution, attached. Historically, some manifestations of it are aborted, while others are diverted from what looks like a predictable course. Still, with this spirit having appeared on the scene, it is reasonable that we look forward to the day it fully manifests itself. This would be the basis for hope.

Indeed, we can begin to think that it is quite possible for children to grow up in a society where they are judged by the contents of their character and not the colour of the skin, their religion, their place of birth, or their parents' ancestry or station in life. Theirs would be a time of social mobility based on merit alone, where status and privileges flow from achievement and not from inherited identities. But before this spirit is fully manifested, even in Canada, our times still have to be demystified and made no longer sacred. We still have to overcome the dream deficit—the difference between the desire and the reality, between the current human condition and the quest for freedom that has brought us this far. We will have to, as the Indian-Canadian sociologist Hirmani Bannerji argues, come to terms with the dark side of the nation, and of each one of us individually.[33]

That this spirit is developing in Canada signals something else about humanity's ongoing quest to create institutions and agencies that will allow people to develop to their highest potential. Undoubtedly, military power and economic well-being—symbols of prosperity and the ability to defend against tyrants—are indicators of how well nations have developed. They are some of our most cherished signs of freedom and independence, and they have long been at the heart of the human quest for a better life. But historically, these indicators have been viewed with suspicion. Indeed, economic and military superiority might just as easily indicate that people have been transformed into the very tyrants from which most of humanity is fleeing.

As the American philosopher Cornell West argues, often there are non-market, and non-battlefield, matters that give greater meaning to our lives. Other social factors are taken into consideration, such as the relations that exist within the state and whether members of society feel that they can freely develop their talents and skills. Indeed, some might even reject military might as anathema to the spirit of humanism that they see at the heart of human development. This book suggests that the Canadian experience of multiculturalism is showing that the northern forces are winning the argument that resulted in the American War of Independence. These are human qualities that are already making Canada, in the parlance of even the American politicians, a "gentler" place in which to live. This is why so many immigrants choose to come to Canada—they want to live and raise their children in a less threatening society, one where they feel more at home.

Developing this line of reasoning, we can argue that Canada continues to mature as a site for sociological, philosophical, and cultural developments. This is a role that Canada started playing in the days of the old British Empire and continues to play in the Commonwealth. The part is acted out internationally and at home, where Canada has set itself up as an example of how a genuinely pluralist society can function effectively. In so doing, it has developed lessons in human social adaptability for sister countries like South Africa and Australia, which have traditionally followed Canada's constitutional lead. Today, both Australia and South Africa continue to follow that lead, abandoning the attempt to create white men's countries and starting instead on a path that is supposed to lead to blindness on matters of colour.

As multicultural states, these two countries are practising colour awareness when it comes to dealing officially with their citizens, even though those citizens may define themselves by their own race or ethnicity. And Canada, Australia, and South Africa have in common something else that was developed first in Canada: all three realized that trying to create a racialized state was a dead end that could only lead to the destruction of the very society they were trying to develop. Their original plans, they realized, could only lead to death and destruction, and even to physical violence from those who were traditionally shut out of the imagination of the nation-state. Canada was the first to switch from a racial dream to its very opposite: the raceless society that is the new spirit taking flight around the globe.

These examples are being copied in other countries that are fast transforming themselves, through immigration and the recognition of ethnic and racial minorities, into multicultural, pluralist societies. We can think, for example, of European countries like Ireland, Italy, Germany, Greece, and Portugal—nation-states that have stopped being net exporters of their people and have become immigrant-receiving countries like Canada. These are countries that must look to the rest of the world to provide many of their current workers and their future citizens—a pattern that has long been at work in Canada. These countries must now find a way, as Canada did, of encouraging these new citizens to think of themselves as a single people—a people noted more for their pluralism, diversity, and difference than for their uniformity. And Canada is also becoming a model for Eastern European countries—those that experts like the political philosopher Will Kymlicka argue could benefit from the importation of Canada's communitarian model of liberal democracy with its emphasis on pluralism.[34] We may yet achieve Modernity's dream of strong individual states whose members cling together not because of race but because of a moral and ethical desire to be together in all our diversity. What would make this exercise a child of Modernity would be a unity of intention to produce a specific state and culture. Otherwise, in content and even form, it would be fragments as diversified as any post-Modern entity.

In new times we find the scraps and residues of old times. But this is not a story lost on history. Time, as Alexander the Great recognized, might have petrified into a great and impenetrable knot, the vines tangled around the ox cart of old in Gordium, but it has never exhausted all solutions. There is always another way worth considering. This is another lesson of history that was not lost on Canada. This is a drama that is still being lived every day. It is a story whose characters have remained the same while its aims and goals have changed. It is a story of struggles, of how the change at the heart of this history is itself now more universally accepted. And it is a story that tells us that our history will end and another will begin, as it did for those who preceded us and thought they were shaping a history for all times, and in that newness our actions and intentions—indeed, our morality—will be judged by the coldness of an amoral history.

chapter two

THE BLACKEST MONTH

February of each new year arrives in the New World with a special magic. Serendipity seems to be at play, and usually it has as its playground the same fields on which the hopes and dreams of this Modern era were first crystallized. This, the front pages of our newspapers and screens of our televisions told us, was the case in the year 2004. This was a special month in a special year, a time when Black history was being both celebrated and acted out, just as was intended in 1926, when a week was first set aside to celebrate and motivate the American "Negro," and to review his marks on the pages of history. Now a full four weeks, Black History Month, and the spirit that gave birth to it, has spread around the globe.

For New World Blacks and Africans, February is contradiction itself—the shortest month of the year, but the longest on hope. February is the magical moment for displaying achievements, for taking libations to honour the spirits of the past, the present, and the future. It's a month when the entire world is pan-African, and in a multicultural country like Canada, it's a time when all people are as symbolically Black and African as they are Irish on St. Patrick's Day. February is a time for many people to remember that they have chosen to place themselves above and beyond the things considered lowly African, and by extension Black, and that they too must be brought low in their thinking to understand more fully the human condition. From the other side of the ledger of history, February is a time that reminds so many people that choices have been made for and about them, and that some of the most painful were based on the belief that they were not entitled to full recognition within the nation-state or to rise as high within the human family as ambition, imagination, and hard work would normally take them.

Still, that spirit of the ages continues moving on, searching for its destination, seeking to fully know itself. Just like the Ol' Man River, it keeps rolling along, lingering now and again to determine what it should raise up, what it should preserve, and what it should carry forward. In February 2004, this spirit, seemingly, was going forward by moving backwards; it was celebrating while weeping. It had settled once again on Haiti, a symbol of both the abjection of the human condition and the human capacity to hope. This is a nation-state whose citizens are marked by the complexion of their skin and the depth of their spirit—a spirit that, in its quest for freedom, historically has mirrored the rest of the world.

Haiti in the year 2004 was a representation of the ambitions and hopes of an individual group of people, and of the trials and tribulations of all peoples. And most of the contradictions came to us graphically, in photographs—of death caused by human hands and the floods of nature; of presidents falling and new ones rising; of learned men and women of countries in the region meeting to determine what they should do about the perennial Haitian question; of Haitians themselves asking to be left to their own devices. To many people, Haiti represents diverse things: the ailing parent whose children have returned home to sit at the bedside, to reminisce and to gather up hope; or the desperate mother who still gathers her children around her and tries to smile again, and to ask them how they are doing on their own in a big, cruel world. Haiti is, contradictorily, both the ailing parent and the prodigal children, who know they are the inheritors of a proud legacy, even if at times they don't want to be associated too closely with the source.

In settling on Haiti in 2004, spirit was inviting all peoples, and all nations, to look within themselves and to compare the ideals they hold with the conditions under which they and their neighbours actually exist. Would they want to exchange positions? To the questions of conscience asked of them by spirit, these people could only answer once again that they are not their brothers' or sisters' keepers, thereby indicting themselves with their own words. The answers could come only out of their sense of morality. Unless we are willing to repeat the errors of the past, these answers could come only out of a history that needs to end. For maybe we are our brothers' and sisters' keepers, and perhaps the damage that we do them is damage done equally to all of us. This is our new morality, a morality on which we may want to construct a new history. For two hundred years, Haiti has been trying, with some success, to give humanity a new narrative, a new vision, and new answers to eternal human problems. It has been trying to tell us all that if there is a need for a nation-state, it is because we are the keepers of our brothers and sisters, and because everyone is a relation. In the nation-state, we may not be a single nation, but at least we can act as if we are one— and as if all members have equal status. For a long time now, Haiti has been urging us to look for new answers to old questions. In what could very well be the ultimate trick of history, this is a message that resonates in Canada, with its ideals of multiculturalism. A country that has historically presented a seemingly dysfunctional Haiti as its *bête noir* is now foremost among those that have accepted the Haitian model of race and ethnic relations. This is a story of note.

WHAT MADE THAT MOMENT in February 2004 different was the complexion of the souls making and reviewing Haiti's history and its future prospects. These men and women—Kofi Annan, Colin

Powell, Condoleeza Rice, and others—had reached heights of power and acclaim in their own nation-states and internationally that were merely dreamed of by their ancestors. For they were of African ancestry and their skin was Black. Arrayed on the world stage next to them were presidents and prime ministers, foreign advisers and technocrats from across the globe—all of them, based on skin colour, Black—people who at one time would have pejoratively been called Haitian, but who now held in their hands the power to decide the future of a still-troubled Haiti and the rest of humanity as well. Even those of a different lineage and pigmentation were metaphorically Black and Haitian as they accepted the legitimacy of the freed members of a purported Black race and acknowledged what freedom has traditionally meant in a Haitian context.

Black or white, these men and women were all asserting the solidarity and inclusiveness of humanity. And in doing this, even if they were acting unintentionally, as vassals of a spirit or a wider morality now called world opinion, they were testifying to the amazing achievements and success of the Haitian Revolution worldwide, and to the eternal hope in the hearts of just about everyone that there is a time a-coming when we will study race no more. For by February 2004, the world had finally recognized that it could not long continue with one part human and the other less than human, one part philosophically Black and the other white, one part culturally advanced and the other developing. These parts had to become, in spirit and by Modernity's imagining, Haitian.

The people of Haiti were once again in a revolutionary mood as February 2004 opened. As *The New York Times* and just about every other newspaper of record noted repeatedly, Haiti is a special place, like the home of a dysfunctional family. Haiti: the poorest nation in the Americas. Haiti: the nation with the highest levels of HIV/AIDS in the Americas. Haiti: the place where a fledgling democracy had produced little more than refugees on U.S. shores, and where elected presidents are not expected to serve out their terms of office.

As *The Guardian* newspaper in London reported in its editorial on February 14, 2004: "Looked at from afar, Haiti is one of those places where the news is usually either bad, or very bad."

"By the time the acrid wisps of smoke reached his nostrils, it was too late for Benjamin Emmanuel to save anything except himself," reported Lydia Polgreen in *The New York Times* on February 12, 2004. "The schoolbooks he used to prepare French lessons for his students would turn to ash. So would the law books that each cost a quarter of his monthly salary, a sum he gladly paid to study a profession that might pay him better." In a seemingly never-ending story of self-inflicted degeneracy, not progress, Haiti has watched all its dreams turn to ashes of one kind or another. This was ultimately a story of death and decay, an unrelenting narrative of unchanging metaphors and people without hope—people whose best days were two hundred years ago in a pre-revolutionary era. Or at least that is the view of a purportedly unerring dominant narrative. This is a place where the future collapses daily into a present that is always worse than the nethermost reaches of the past. Haiti, as James Anthony Froude had claimed as far back as 1886, is a place where you smell the stench—a fetid mixture of decay and fecundity, of ashes to ashes and dust to dust—from miles away.

For all of Black History Month in the year marking the bicentenary of Modernity's arrival, the spirit of freedom had returned to its nativity crib in Haiti. The eyes of the world were on this mythological piece of Africa in the Caribbean, and on the children of that great revolution, who are still trying to sort out the mess that is as much an inheritance as a bad legacy. If a picture tells a thousand words, then volumes were contained in the snapshots coming out of Haiti, a country that, depending on your point of view, is either the beginning or the end of history.

In February 2004, what was presumed to be a second Haitian Revolution was simmering. This time, the revolt targeted a ruler who was considered by some a despot and a modern-day slavemaster, by others a modern-day saviour, the embodiment of their hopes and of democracy. The spirit of the times had found one man to personify its many contradictions. But if a tyrant, he was different from the ones whose overthrow during the Haitian Revolution of 1804 shook the world to its very foundations; if a saviour, he was as important as a Moses or an Ogun for those who were still struggling, exactly two hundred years after the great revolution, to cash its promissory notes.

For one thing, the colour of this great man's skin was different from that of the tyrants of old: Jean-Bertrand Aristide was Black and a son of the soil, a product of the very revolution that had earned his country both infamy and praise. And just as important, this modern-day liberator was the same colour as those in the initial revolution. His Blackness was part of the legacy of hope for two groups of people who were linked in the same struggle, even if the times and appearances had changed. Both sides claimed as their legacy the constitution that was proclaimed a year after the Haitian Revolution. Both sides were claiming this inheritance.

This was only the third written constitution—after the American and the French—in the Modern world, a document that proclaimed the hopes and dreams of a people. That it even existed at all was a testament to how far a group of mainly Black-skinned rebels had come in overthrowing the existing social and political order. In an act of political will that captured the spirit of their times, they had declared themselves freed men and women, fully human, and citizens of a great land. They were no longer slaves. They were no longer left outside the Modern state, whose main task was to perfect humans and to give them a culture and a wider sense of civilization. These former slaves, who were once from Africa, declared themselves to be a new state, Hayti. "In our name," the constitution proclaimed, "as in that of the people of Hayti, who have legally constituted us faithfully organs and interpreters of their will, in the presence of the Supreme Being, before whom all mankind are equal, and who has scattered so many species of creatures on the surface of the earth for the purpose of manifesting his glory and his power by the diversity of his work, in the presence of all nature by whom we have been so unjustly and for so long a time considered as outcast children." Like the American and French constitutions, this was one of Modernity's birth certificates.

The revolution challenged the notion that some people are better employed working for a so-called superior group, and that the different groups should be allowed to develop exclusive homelands of nations and states where they would produce their own cultures and determine what is good for them. It rejected the notion that inferior and superior groups are incapable of producing the same culture, working towards the same goals, and sharing a unified purpose and intent. Indeed, even as an act of violence, the Haitian Revolution was an attempt to show that humanity's natural state did not involve separate and unique groups constantly at war because of incompatible interests, aspirations, concerns, and cultures.

But the Haitian document, penned in 1805, was revolutionary and groundbreaking in a way that exceeded the American and French constitutions and that still captures the spirit and general will of peoples around the globe: it sought to include all those who'd been excluded, either in theory or in practice, from the nation-states created by the French and American documents. Haiti's was a revolution in the truest sense of the word, for its goal was to subvert and radically overthrow all the commonly held assumptions that emerged with the birth of identity and the rise of individual culture at the beginning of Modernity. It set out not to establish a white nation but to reaffirm a Black one. It set out not to exclude, except for those who considered themselves superior, but to mend humanity's rifts. And as the nineteenth article of the constitution made clear, the symbolism of hope was to be obvious. "The national colours," it proclaimed, "shall be black and red."

Unlike Modernity's two previous documents, this constitution was concerned less with the physical appearances of unity—the unity that comes, for example, from having people of an exclusive ethnicity in a nation-state—and more with the spirit and intentions of different peoples to live as one and to produce a single way of life or a single culture. Inner desires for good trumped outer manifestations. The document sought to celebrate the diversity of people scattered around the globe (all of whom were capable of inclusion if in the right spirit), and it sought to bring the outcast children of Modern times into a homeland that would be accepting of them. "Slavery is forever abolished," the document said in its second article, making the liberation of all humanity the first act of the new nation-state. This first act would begin the battle against race.

Both the American and the French documents were concerned primarily with the freedom of a people. There remained a racial and ethnic distinction, in the imagining behind these documents, between humanity in general and "a people," meaning those who would become the nation-state. The first article of the avant-garde Haitian constitution, by contrast, vowed to set up "a free state, sovereign and independent of any power in the universe." In its third article, the constitution declared who was entitled to be included in this new state. "The Citizens of Hayti," it said, emphasizing universal solidarity, "are brothers at home; equality in the eyes of the law is incontestably acknowledged, and there cannot exist any titles, advantages, or privileges, other than those necessarily resulting from the consideration and reward rendered to liberty and independence." (As a document of its time, the constitution used the term "brothers" to stand for all humanity.) Finally, the constitution claimed, "The law is the same to all, whether it punishes, or whether it protects."

These were its universal ideals for inclusiveness and its aims to eliminate social inequalities. But the constitution also addressed matters of exclusion. "No whiteman of whatever nation he may be," the document read, "shall put his foot on this territory with the title of master or proprietor, neither shall he in future acquire any property therein." This did not include white women, who with their children automatically became naturalized Haytians. Of course, any white men coming in peace and without aspirations to enslave were welcomed.

The constitution also indicated which people would be genuine and natural citizens—and in a way that put the issue beyond doubt. With the accepting "of [mixed] colour among the children of one and the same family … the Haytian shall hence forward be known only by the generic appellation of Black." Black was not solely a colour of skin—it was the reflection of a mind that had good and pure intentions to all humans. The opposite of this was the person who had an impure heart or bad intentions towards other humans. According to the revolutionary view of the world, such an individual, regardless of gender or colour of skin, was a "whiteman." In other words, even naturalized white women, and white Germans and Poles, as we'll see in a moment, were Black if they were Haitian citizens. Colour of skin did not matter. What did matter was that they were human, and what made them human was that they did not set themselves apart from the rest of humanity or hold fellow humans in bondage.

Naturalized Germans and "Polanders" were singled out in the constitution. These were men who were driven by their essential humanity rather than the colour of their skin. By fighting for the victorious revolutionaries, they proved to all Haitians they were distinct from the whitemen who wanted to treat others as physical property. The whiteman concerned himself with the particular, or what is called the contingent manifestation of a particular interest. He was not interested in what is universal and unchanging for all humanity.

In addition, the constitution upheld property rights in general, claiming that "property is sacred, [and] its violation shall be severely prosecuted." In this, it was as much a liberal bourgeoisie document as the constitutions of the American and French revolutions. But it did make a distinction in determining what constituted property—and it made clear that humans were not the property of other humans. The highest form of ownership was self-ownership, and citizenship was the highest identity an individual could attain within the nation-state. Citizenship guaranteed that an individual's rights would be recognized by the nation-state, and it also affirmed that individuals who owned themselves had an "inalienable" right to belong within the state and to be recognized as equal—that is, not superior or inferior—to all other citizens. White Frenchmen, meanwhile, were to lose their property because of a double strike against them: they were the former slaveowners, and they had been the enemies of the revolution that brought this new state into being. They were excluded on these grounds, which made them "whitemen," and not simply because of their white skin. It is worth pointing out that the Haitian constitution seemed to suggest that all nations of the globe had their share of whitemen, those who would hold fellow citizens, and fellow humans, in physical bondage. To be a whiteman was to be a dastardly person, even if the skin was any colour of the rainbow.

This distinction is important. The Haitian constitution was novel in its approach to property. In the rest of the Americas, the dominant philosophy held that the civil state was a place where people owned property. Indeed, John Locke said that we can determine citizenship through the ownership of property—those with it were achieving their potential, while those without were not on the same level. Under this philosophy, it was accepted that African slaves in the Americas not only did not own property but were not yet fully human. Indeed, they were owned as property by those who had already achieved full humanity through the possession of other objects with economic value. This is why African slaves—called Negroes and, more derogatorily, niggers—were considered to be two-thirds human. They were on their way to being perfected in a civil society, but they did not possess that final third of humanity that was expressed through the ownership of physical property. Worse, they were called coons—for raccoons, with their black faces and wide eyes edged by white—one of the most insulting and degrading of all caricatures of Blacks, especially those regarded as uppity and disrespectful of whites. As the cultural theorist Donald Bogle explains, in his study of images of Blacks in Modernity, "The pure coon emerged as no-account niggers, those unreliable, crazy, lazy subhuman creatures good for nothing more than eating water-melons, stealing chickens, shooting crap, or butchering the English language."[1] We will want to recall this negative image of Blacks when we look again at the word "coon" and the position it held in the dominant literary imagination in Canada in chapter three.

The Haitian Revolution contested these principles. It argued that all human beings were equal, whether they owned physical property or not. It then went further and said that one human being, regard-less of social status, could not be the property of another. Any human being who owned another had no place in a society intended for the betterment and advancement of all its members. Humans who owned other humans were setting themselves up as whitemen, the type of beings Aristotle had described as gods or barbarians who had no need for society (which took its highest form in the nation-state). Such people were not amenable to the socialization and equality of treatment for which the nation-state is intended. In effect, the Haitian revolutionaries argued that a nation-state could not exist with half its members treated as humans and the other half as property; it could not exist with one stratum of society whose members were like gods and another whose members were chattel. The ideal state, therefore, could not be based on race, as so many of Modernity's leading thinkers were suggesting.

Time was on the side of the Haitian philosophers. Six decades later, the leader of another embattled nation-state would appear in a cemetery to explain why his country was being racked by a civil war. "Four score and seven years ago our fathers brought forth on this continent a new nation, conceived in liberty, and dedicated to the proposition that all men are created equal. Now we are engaged in a great civil war, testing whether that nation, or any nation so conceived and so dedicated, can long endure." This was how Abraham Lincoln began his famous Gettysburg Address, a speech in which he argued that a civil war was needed for the United States of America to be able to live up to its intentions and goals. "It is rather for us to be here dedicated to the great task remaining before us—that from these honored dead we take increased devotion to that cause for which they gave the last full measure of devotion—that we here highly resolve that these dead shall not have died in vain, that this nation, under God, shall have a new birth of freedom—and that government of the people, by the people, for the people shall not perish from the earth."

Lincoln had formalized a new meaning for the theory and prac-tice of democracy. The Civil War was being fought, he averred, so that those held as mere property, as not cultured enough to be considered full citizens, would be brought completely into the nation-state. In seeking to fill the gaps of the American Revolution, Lincoln had adopted the philosophy of the Haitian revolutionaries, who had argued that a nation-state could not consist of Black people and "whitemen."

Once again, however, history appeared to have played one of its tricks. We may recall that many Black-skinned Haitians had fought for the ideals of the American Revolution and then were disap-pointed that the liberty promised by that revolution did not extend to Africans and Blacks. Many of them took their quest for freedom back to Haiti, where they became the mentors of the successful Haitian revolutionaries. Having established a beachhead in Haiti, the spirit of freedom then returned to the United States to fill in the gaps left by the American Revolution. The fight for freedom had come full circle. Its goals were to free all humanity and to break the power of those who owned other humans—or were, in the Haitian sense, whitemen.

One hundred years later, Martin Luther King, Jr., would cement this thinking in a speech that is now recited around the world as a paean to racelessness. In this speech, he talked about the inhumanity and lack of advancement that were the common lot of another racialized group of people—those whose ancestry was African and whose skin was Black. He lamented that even in the 1960s, they were not counted as fully human and covered by the American constitution's claim that all men are created equal. He said:

> So we've come here today to dramatize a shameful condition. In a sense we've come to our nation's capital to cash a check. When the architects of our republic wrote the magnificent words of the Constitution and the Declaration of Independence, they were signing a promissory note to which every American was to fall heir.
>
> This note was a promise that all men would be guaranteed the unalienable rights of life, liberty, and the pursuit of happiness.
>
> It is obvious today that America has defaulted on this promissory note insofar as her citizens of color are concerned. Instead of honoring this sacred obligation, America has given the Negro people a bad check, a check that has come back marked "insufficient funds."
>
> But we refuse to believe that the bank of justice is bankrupt. We refuse to believe that there are insufficient funds in the great vaults of opportunity of this nation. And so we've come to cash this check, a check that will give us upon demand the riches of freedom and the security of justice. We have also come to this hallowed spot to remind America of the fierce urgency of now. This is no time to engage in the luxury of cooling off

or to take the tranquilizing drug of gradualism. Now is the time to make real the promises of democracy. Now is the time to rise from the dark and desolate valley of segregation to the sunlit path of racial justice. Now is the time to lift our nation from the quicksands of racial injustice to the solid rock of brotherhood. Now is the time to make justice a reality for all of God's children.

On that day in 1963, the aims King espoused were no different from those advocated by the Haitian revolutionaries.

ARISING OUT OF THIS HISTORY and this hope is one other act of note that occurred in February 2004. This was an event of global importance, a symbol (for in our real world, we also live by symbols and metaphor—ultimately they allow us to bring meaning to our lives) of the folly that can overtake the human imagination, of how often humans, thinking they are all-powerful, unleash forces that spin out of their control and produce evil and harm beyond what was intended. This was the symbolism of a kind of nation building that is different from the Haitian revolutionary model just described.

This was the situation that faced the most powerful military nation-state in the world. With the help of a few other Western partners, primarily Britain and Spain, the United States of America had invaded and conquered Iraq almost a year earlier. The invasion went against world opinion, but in a few short weeks, the Iraqi military had been overrun, the government overthrown, and the country was a de facto colony of the United States and its coalition partners. A provisional government was charged with the task of quickly establishing a new administration, with the hope of restoring sovereignty to Iraq. The game seemed over for the old regime when its leader, Saddam Hussein, first lost his two sons, Uday and Qusay, and then was himself pulled from a hole in the ground where he was sheltering. Images flashed on television screens around the globe. They showed a broken man, evidence of how the mighty can be brought low, and of the speed and accuracy of the technology that had made the United States almost a god unto itself. The country appeared to have the technology to overcome anything, including distance, time, and human obstacles.

But at another level, the script was not working out as planned. Many Iraqis were not accepting the conquest as easily as the super-power had predicted before the invasion. They were fighting back, destabilizing the new government. Faced with what looked like a growing quagmire, the leader of the most powerful nation-state in the world turned to the only agency he felt was capable of saving his country from its own machinations. This was the United Nations, the embodiment of the global morality that is expressed as world opinion and the modern-day successor to the League of Nations. In making its case for war in Iraq, the United States had previously ignored the spirit of the world, as expressed by the U.N., and suggested that the global body was fast becoming irrelevant to the story of human progress and achievement.

Power and morality rested with a particular country that had on its own decided what was right and what was wrong, and that had the ability to back up its opinion with deadly force. Its representative took to the podium of the U.N. to lecture its members on the danger of the organization's losing its place and position in a new world order that the United States was prepared to fashion on its own. Iraq would be but one piece in this puzzle. Soon, the good old boys would be drinking whisky and rye and celebrating with slices of their favourite pie.

But at what should have been the height of its victory, the United States seemed instead like a massive Gulliver bound to the ground by the Lilliputians of the invaded country. At the time of its announced irrelevance, the United Nations looked triumphant. In February 2004, the world waited for a decision from a man who appeared to be the embodiment not of the highest military and economic powers but of the world's morality and integrity. The United States of America, in all its hubris as the sole remaining superpower, had turned to the United Nations for help in extricating itself from what some were calling its latest Vietnam.

The symbolism of this struggle was the real meaning of what Modernity has become. At the head of the United Nations was Kofi Annan, the secretary-general, who was decried as a weakling. Those who felt he had not done enough to prevent the war claimed he was a puppet of the mighty United States, while those who favoured the war claimed he was unwilling to make the tough decisions needed to make the world a safer place. In the end, it would be up to Annan to decide the conditions under which the world body would oversee the elections that would allow the United States to start its face-saving exit from Iraq.

At least one other actor in this drama was important, and although he'd left the centre stage of world opinion, he still commanded much moral sway. This was the South African revolutionary Nelson Mandela, arguably the world's favourite moral son. Mandela was a former prisoner who brought the apartheid regime of Smuts, Wilson, and the Canadians Laurier and Mackenzie King to the ground, and then became president of South Africa, a citizen of the world, and an honorary Canadian. Then eighty-four years old, Mandela had criticized George Bush over the invasion of Iraq. In just about every magazine, newspaper, and newscast worldwide, the man who was described as "maybe the world's most respected statesmen" by *Newsweek* magazine had called the American president racist and said the war was a racist one.[2] Then he went a step further, alleging that the Americans' treatment of the United Nations was also racist, for they would not have behaved as they did if a white man was the secretary-general.

Kofi Annan, like Mandela, is a Nobel laureate for peace. Both are also Africans and have Black skin. And here stand the contradictions of Modernity. As Blacks and Africans, they are symbolic of the diminished role in humanity's advancement Modernity had originally intended for all who look like them. But at the same time, they are symbols of what has gone wrong with Modernity, of how it has both lost its way and forfeited a great moral battle. This is a war that humanity, in general, has won. This is a turn in Modernity's attempts to show that there can still be unity in differences. And when people who look like Annan and Mandela step onto the world's stage, they show how race has changed the world and is changing itself.

As Annan and Mandela discussed what would be morally right for the world, for the United States of America, and for Iraq, they were often in conversation with people who looked so much like them. They were in a struggle for moral dominance with people whose skins are as Black as theirs. For facing off against them, representing the powerful United States, were two people with different viewpoints and moralities. Colin Powell, the U.S. secretary of state, and Condoleeza Rice, the national security adviser, were part of the power behind the throne that is the president of the United States. Significantly, for practical and programmatic purposes, as well as moral legitimacy, the world's most dominant country must now show to the world at least one Black face as part of this power complex. Perhaps this is hypocrisy, but it is nevertheless what is now expected as a norm of good behaviour. The image that shot around the world was of four Black-skinned people having a moral disagreement on a matter of pivotal importance to the entire world. More important than the discussion itself was that what they thought mattered to world affairs—and ultimately to history.

When Powell and Rice were in school, there were no Blacks holding their positions, not because they were not worthy intellectually, but because they were considered morally unfit and representative of a different culture and civilization. This judgment was based on one factor: the colour of their skin. Blacks were deemed not to be representative of the right race—a judgment that would have applied to Annan and Mandela at one time too. Instead, people who looked like these characters from Modernity's newest play would have been counting the achievements of others who, though they might have been of a totally different morality, nevertheless represented every Black when they first appeared on television, won a heavyweight fight, got elected to any national or international position, or stepped from behind a boundary to take their position at the cricket crease or batter's plate.

But the times had changed—and with them the exclusions and limits race had imposed on sections of humanity. As part of the change, the perceived race of men and women in national and international affairs supposedly does not now matter. Morality and the shaping of ethical orders in the nation and around the world have escaped the surly bonds that tied them to the preconception that some people are naturally inferior and others superior. Not only were the times a-changing, but the symbols were too. Indeed, what we have been discussing may be more signs of a time when, in fulfillment of this trend, race will not matter. But it took humanity some time and many struggles to get to the point where we can entertain even greater hopes. And from the very beginning, Haiti was always in the mix.

IN ONE INSTANT, the deed was done and Modernity's latest model of the state was established. Unlike the earlier versions of the Americans and the French, this model was intended to fight against the racism of exclusion. The new nation-state was intended for all humanity, not just those who acted as gods or tyrants. It was to be a place where people would find refuge, peace, and the conditions that would allow them to live long in the land. Under this model, the state was made for humans, not the other way around. Membership in the state was not to be determined among supposedly racialized categories of humans the world over.

The very act of trying to set up a raceless society was racial. It involved determining who should be recognized as a citizen and on what basis that recognition would occur. In the case of Haiti, Black was presented as racially and morally superior. The unhyphenated whiteman (defined as a particular category of humans who kept others in slavery) was inferior and excluded. Those in this category were not fighting for the wider interest of all humans. They were not on the side of the good guys, and thus were deemed to be evil in thoughts and actions. Only the particularists and the narrow-minded were to be excluded. This state was to be home, symbolically, to all others.

Haiti would be Black because Black and African people, as defined in the original constitution, were in the majority. This was a version of the one-drop rule that Modernity had given to the world—the idea that any mixing of white and Black inevitably produced Blackness, degrading the ideals of purity and whiteness. The state was also based on the idea that Black was not only a skin colour but, as proven by the Germans, Poles, and naturalized white women mentioned in the constitution, a commitment, a culture, and a way of life.

By Modernity's measure, any nation-state with non-white people would be viewed as Black and in keeping with the model set by the Haitian Revolution. Standing in opposition to the Black nations would be the white ones—those that were promised by Modernity's two other great revolutions, the American and the French. Indeed, the French Revolution produced both a new republican state and a colonial France, in which Black and African colonies were still treated as inferior in an empire of different peoples and supposedly different races.

Haiti's achievements were many. It was the first independent Black republic in the world, the first independent Black republic in the Americas, and the titular homeland of all freedom-loving Black people. The Haitian Revolution also completed the process started by the American and French revolutions, bringing men and women from all backgrounds into the nation-state. In this sense, the Haitian Revolution was the main revolution that started Modernity. It was the first attempt at official multiculturalism. Unfortunately, the main spokespeople of Modernity did not recognize multiculturalism as their goal. Instead, they wanted the opposite: a country that was as homogeneous as possible. They wanted to erase differences and diversities, assimilating them into the archetypal Frenchman or American boy of Modernity. Other nation-states would follow in these footsteps, adopting the same plans and strategies for nation building—making this spirit of Modernity pervasive. That they did not achieve their goal is the story of their disappointment. Yet this is also the story of the triumph of those who were not originally considered part of the plans of those developing nation-states. In the end, plurality, so symbolic of the differences and diversity in the human family, trumped homogeneity in nation building.

What the American and French revolutions did not resolve was who was to be free in the nation-state. Common men had fought for recognition and rights in the state that would emerge from the French republic—a state built on the belief that all human beings could be made noble in society, and that they should have the liberty to live freely and to achieve their full potential regardless of the conditions under which they were born. A new spirit and culture could be instilled in them in the state. Similarly, the American Revolution was predicated on the notion that all men (and, supposedly, women) were created equal and endowed with inalienable rights.

These rights were guaranteed in the new society, which was the American nation-state. But there was one glaring anomaly in the protestations of both the American and the French revolutionaries: human beings were being held in physical slavery within territories they claimed as part of their nation-states. Did these humans not have a right to expect freedom, recognition and inclusion in the state, and liberty, equality, and fraternity, so that they could be prosperous and happy? Slavery was the snake in the grass for both these nation-states. Modernity's project was incomplete, or it was determining that a large proportion of humanity had no place in the nation-state.

Some of these people were enslaved in the part of France then called Santo Domingo and later called Hayti (or Haiti). Greater numbers were enslaved on the American mainland and in neighbouring countries that the U.S. hoped to influence, countering the sway of European powers in the region. But the Haitian Revolution showed that African and Black-skinned people could have nation-states of their own, and that they could have a presence and be accepted as full citizens in any other nation-state of the world. This revolution showed that the model offered by Modernity to European and white-skinned peoples could be adapted to suit the needs and desires of other peoples as well. The Haitian Revolution was needed to fix the flaws in its American and French counter-parts. It aimed to give all peoples the right of sovereignty, either as individuals or within a nation-state of their choosing. With that, a significant part of Modernity's project to free the individual subject was in place. Haiti had given Modernity real freedom by allowing real individual choices. And the result was a project that reached into the lived reality of every entity that thought of itself as a nation-state of free individuals.

In Brazil, this led to the popular form of government termed "racial democracy." In 1888, Brazil had become politically independent, ending slavery one step ahead of a revolution by the African-Brazilian population, the largest group of people of African ancestry in a single country in the Americas. Brazil's racial democracy, which grew out of the Haitian model, was one of the earliest attempts at multiculturalism, although Brazil was not officially recognized as a multicultural country. The Haitian model was also the basis for several democratic governments that former slaves and their descendants tried to set up in the British Caribbean. In these governments the colour of the skin would not matter and the majority would rule, regardless of the majority's skin colour.

The Haitian Revolution startled whites and Europeans the world over, especially those the constitution recognized as "white-men." But, contradictorily, the revolution would become the argu-ment for exclusive white *and* Black nation-states, and finally for the racial democracies that were the forerunners of what we now call multiculturalism. It would also be celebrated in The Haitian Trilogy, three plays written by a son of the revolution who would go on to become a Nobel laureate for literature.

Derek Walcott was born in St. Lucia. If he has a particular affil-iation, it would be to St. Lucia or the English-speaking Caribbean, an affiliation he shares with those from nations like Jamaica, Trinidad, Guyana, Barbados, and the Bahamas. These islands contained within them the kernel of a greater union called the Caribbean community, an arrangement that is based on the notion that several islands of the Caribbean are at heart one nation, even if they have the political trappings of independent and distinct countries. Somewhere in the future is the hope for a final union where the predominantly Black peoples of the region would become one nation-state. Theirs would be a Black nation in concept, even if it was described as "plural" or "mixed."

Most of the Caribbean Common Market countries had once formed a West Indies political federation, an ill-fated alliance that Walcott celebrated by penning *Drums and Colours* in 1958, on the opening of the first parliament in Trinidad. This play was the second in The Haitian Trilogy, which aimed to tell the wider story of the four-hundred-year history of the entire region, and Haiti's central role in this narrative of war, conquest, rebellion, and nationhood. By then, Walcott, like so many other Caribbean peoples since the Haitian Revolution, had recognized that he was Haitian even though he was not native to that land. The spirit of Haiti, its focus on inde-pendence and self-determination for all regardless of background, was infused in people like Walcott at birth, giving them a common identity and awareness supposedly based on their African genes and the colour of their skin. But in many respects, the thinking that led to a West Indies federation was no different from Garvey's plans for a United States of Black Africa and Froude's and Smuts's push for a white homeland. Indeed, some suggest that the West Indies federation failed because it was an idea hatched in the Colonial Office in London, and therefore it did not rise up out of the people with the fervour the Haitians had for their revolution and republic.

In the years following the Haitian Revolution, all men and women of African ancestry, and having Black skin, were thought to be Haitian, just as today, in places like New York, London, Toronto, and Paris, natives from all English-speaking Caribbean countries are thought to be Jamaican. This echoed the long-held notions that all Black-skinned people were Ethiopian or Abyssinian. Simply put, for good or evil, to be Black was to be symbolically Haitian. But being Haitian also meant something more for Blacks: being free and independent. Conversely, in earlier times, Black people were said to be Jamaican if they were considered by their white masters more civil and accommodating of other humans, and therefore more worthy of living in a white man's society. They were presented in this imagining as more "civilized" than Haitians—not as likely to fight for their independence and rights of self-determination. But how names and labels have changed with time! In many metropolitan areas, Jamaicans are now considered to be in spirit what the Haitians were generations ago.

"Though in Kingston as elsewhere in Jamaica there are gradations in colour from pure black to pure white, stock of mixed origin is not conspicuous," wrote the Canadian James Mackintosh Bell, a fellow of the Geological Society, the Royal Geographic Society, and the Royal Society of Canada. Bell was writing in 1931, in a book called *Far Places,* an anthropological examination of strange people in places that are physically and perceptually far away from the purported mainstream of Western civilization. His books, which also included *The Wilds of Mooriland, Tales of Red Children,* and *Sidelights on the Siberian Campaign,* tried, as Froude's books did, to describe to people "back home" journeys into the wilds or, in the case of Jamaica, what could safely be called the half-wilds. Bell, like Froude and others, was used to identifying and fixing people with exactness based on their physical appearance.

"Most of the population seems to be almost unadulterated negro," Bell reported. "Yet there are subtle differentiations which the visitor should not ignore. A few days after our arrival a tailor who showed little trace of any but black blood came to try on a coat he was making for me. By way of conversation as he fitted the sleeves I said to him, 'Is it not extraordinary how one finds Scotchmen everywhere?' 'Yes,' he replied, happy at the allusion to the typically Scottish name he bore. As he made a chalk mark here, inserted a pin there, he extolled the merits of the race—finishing with the remark, 'I have a little Hebrew in me, too.' It was only when he had completed his adjustment and was reviewing his handiwork that he added, 'And some African also.'"

As self-identifying Jamaicans of today are likely to say in that ambiguously ambiguous way of theirs: "Cho, 'im too facety. Serve him right!" leaving us to discern to whom the brickbat or salute was intended. Identities are fluid and often defy skin colour and presumed blood type. Bell, an anthropologist worth his salt and aware of the times in which he worked and played, should have facetiously recognized his tailor as a Haitian in spirit, though he had a Scottish name and lived in Jamaica. Seriously, the universalizing spirit of freedom does not respect territorial boundaries established by mere men and women. Identity cannot be tailor-made this easily.

In this way of thinking, the Haitian was also the "Negro" slave struggling for freedom throughout what would fondly become known in the Western hemisphere as the Black Atlantic. He or she would revolt against slavery in Brazil, Cuba, Argentina, and the southern United States, demanding political independence in these countries. Brazil got that independence in 1888, and Cuba followed in 1898. And after several decades of agitation, political independence came, starting in the 1960s, to all those Haitians living in the British Caribbean and all those revolutionaries struggling for liberation and against racial apartheid in South Africa. They would be both Africans and Haitians too.

But Modernity had also produced the white-state model for those who feared or disdained Black power or so-called mixed-race democracy where power is shared by ethnic groups. This model argued that Black-skinned people should have no meaningful role in society. They should be kept out physically or, if they were already within the borders of the territory of the state, held in rigid subjugation. They should be kept on the lower levels of society, on the periphery of power, and held in a caste-like arrangement from generation to generation.

The prototype of this model was developed in Canada. Later, it was refined into official apartheid in South Africa. Neither of these models was democratic or accepted the notion that non-European peoples should be included in the concept of "we the people," which is considered central to the formation of a state. Neither model accepted the notion of majority rule, where decisions would be based on the views, desires, and intentions of most of the people in a democracy. Neither model was a meritocracy, and both instead promoted the belief that abilities and virtues were strictly inherited and could be developed only among people with similar genetic and cultural backgrounds. Each was elitist, oligarchic, and autocratic. Each believed in controlling the motion of its people—Canada with the passport and South Africa with the passbook. Each took it for granted that to be white was to be privileged, and that privileges and entitlements were automatically the right of the whites of society. And in both cases, Haiti (and Haitians themselves) was presented as the extreme, as what these nation-states (and their citizens) did not want to become.

MUCH HAD HAPPENED by the time the people of Haiti found themselves caught up in a new fervour at the beginning of their revolutionary bicentenary in 2004. It had been two hundred years since Haiti's independence, but also ten years since South Africa had become symbolically Haitian, and therefore the Black president of South Africa was on hand for Haiti's bicentennial celebrations. Indeed, it seemed as if the spirits had conspired. Together, both countries celebrated their independence and freedom as Black nation-states—states in which every citizen was idealistically treated as racially the same. How the times have changed! There, at the rostrum of the National Palace in Port-au-Prince, stood the leaders of two countries that had once represented two irreconcilable notions of state formation. Marcus Garvey would not have dreamt of such a sight. "South Africa," he said in 1929, "is a hotbed of trouble between the natives who are black and the colonists who are European. There are two million Europeans in and around the Union of South Africa with more than six million natives. These two million have been trying to rob the entire South Africa from the natives who originally owned the country. This leaves no room for goodwill between the two peoples. What the outcome will be, only God can tell."[3]

Before the two leaders stretched an ocean of flag-waving supporters, above them a banner reading, "A Bicentennial of Freedom, for a Millennium of People." The host of the event spoke of history. Haiti, said President Jean-Bertrand Aristide, "was the geographic pivot for black freedom." In the same breath, he hailed the bicentenary of the purchase of the state of Louisiana from France. In the two hundred years since that purchase, many Black and white Americans had considered making Louisiana, as it now exists as a state, the exclusive homeland for Blacks in the United

States. This was an idea that resonated with several African-American intellectuals and separatist groups, including the Nation of Islam and the Black Panthers, and with Abraham Lincoln, the president who took the United States into its gravest crisis, a war to decide if the "nation can for long continue as half free and half slave." Louisiana, which is still considered by many to be the Blackest state of the union, has given so much to the culture and history of the U.S. It has been the capital of the so-called Black Atlantic, a port for African and Black people throughout the region, as well as a place of creolization and hybridity from the mixing of languages—English, French, Spanish, Dutch, aboriginal—used by the Black traders and seamen who linked the Americas in one economic union. Louisiana: the French factor in the United States. So similar to Quebec, the French factor in Canada, and the Afrikaner culture in South Africa's Natal and Cape provinces. At the time it was brought into the American union, Louisiana stretched all the way from the Mississippi River to the Pacific Ocean. It was also the foothold that the French were planning to use for their imperial expansion in North America. Defeat at the hands of Haitian slaves put an end to French ambitions, however, and this defeat signalled a turn in U.S. history that brought race permanently to the forefront of the agenda for nation-state development. After the Louisiana Purchase, the U.S. could expand only through ordered pairs of states, admitting one state that favoured slavery alongside one that was against it. This way, the delicate balance between states was maintained, determining the future of the federal republic. This remained the case until President Lincoln chose to settle the issue of expansion by force through the Civil War. "The United States without Louisiana," Aristide claimed, "would not be the United States."

But just as important to the proceedings as Aristide was the man at his side, Thabo Mbeki, the president of South Africa and the leader of the historic African National Congress, which had fought for a raceless state for most of the twentieth century. Mbeki was the only head of state among the twenty-four foreign representatives on hand for the celebration on the first day of Haiti's bicentenary year. With him were his wife, Zanele, and his foreign minister, Nkosazana Dlamini-Suma, testament to the importance placed on the event by South Africa, an emerging powerhouse in international affairs. And there we had another snapshot worth thousands of words: two men from countries that Modernity had positioned as opposing models for state formation ended up sharing the same stage and celebrating the one model that was valid. The Haitian Revolution had triumphed psychologically, if not economically and politically.

Before leaving his homeland for Haiti, Mbeki had indicated why he was attending. "The celebration of the bicentenary of the Haitian Revolution and the Decade of Liberation in South Africa during the same year, 2004, must serve to inspire Africans to act together, decisively, to end their poverty, underdevelopment, dehumanisation and marginalisation," he said. "As the 1805 Constitution of Haiti said, we have been given 'an opportunity of breaking our fetters, and of constituting ourselves a people, free, civilized and independent'— the opportunity to achieve the African Renaissance."

In pointing out the link between the states in Africa and an island in the Caribbean that has long been viewed as a piece of Africa, Mbeki noted, "As Africans at home—and the diaspora—we must celebrate the victory of 1804, and the inspiring struggle that led to this history success, as part of the process of reasserting our dignity. We must also draw the lesson from this experience that as the African slaves of Haiti succeeded in defeating three of the great European imperial powers of the time, so can we defeat the challenge of poverty and underdevelopment that confronts Africans everywhere." But Mbeki also noted that on several fronts, the Haitian Revolution had been a failure. Haiti is today one of the poorest countries in the world, and it continues to be afflicted by political instability and a failure to maintain democracy. "Its immediate and urgent task, which our countries share," he said, "is to address these challenges. In 1804, independent Haiti was isolated and could not implement the progressive socio-economic changes brought about by the American and French revolutions. Today she shares the common globe with other sister African republics and states."

Referring to those who'd criticized his government's decision to give ten million rand of aid to Haiti, Mbeki said that they "don't know anything about the bicentennial," and its meaning to Africans, Haitians, and Blacks throughout the world. Even harsher reproaches were levelled at critics within South Africa by the country's deputy foreign affairs minister, Aziz Pahad. "For [the critics], the current challenges facing the people of Haiti feed into their stereotype tendency to portray Africans and black people in the continent and elsewhere in the diaspora as hopeless and failures." He added, "We refuse to be party to efforts that seek to obliterate the history and achievements of African people in the continent and elsewhere in the diaspora."

Mbeki seemed justified in talking about his country's leading a renaissance in Africa and in the Black diaspora. An item in *The Sunday Times* of South Africa, published within a few days of Mbeki's statement on Haiti, pointed to a growing trend—the return to South Africa of those who had fled because they thought the country could no longer be their homeland. "They emigrated six or ten years ago fearful of their security and their future or, more recently, attracted by prospects in London or Toronto," the newspaper reported. "But now some are coming back. With little fanfare, but with enthusiasm, white South Africans are returning little by little to a country 'that works' and a homeland they miss. The 'Homecoming Revolution' is on the move." (The Homecoming Revolution is the name of a non-governmental organization that has used the Internet to help expatriates of South Africa make their way back home.) "For the past year," the article continued, "the organization has been the echo chamber for tens of thousands of homesick South Africans, the majority of them white, who found what they thought were greener pastures in Canada or Australia, in Manchester or New York, but are now asking themselves whether leaving was really the right choice."

Choices can be like a double-edged sword, and that appeared to be the case for the spirit that was abroad in the bicentenary of the Haitian Revolution. In Haiti, violence was on the rise as rebels tried to start a new revolution to bring peace, liberty, equality, and fraternity, and to remove Aristide from the Haitian presidency. The day after the public appearance by Mbeki and Aristide, rebels in the northwestern city of Gonaives fired on the helicopter carrying the South African president's advance protection team. As a result, Mbeki had to cancel a planned visit to that part of the country. And in South Africa, too, spirit seemed ambivalent in its feeling towards Blacks—even appeared to be more accepting of whites. AIDS and HIV-infections were among the problems taking their toll on mainly the Black population. But in keeping with Modern tradition, Canada was the country talking loudest about the need to combat this scourge, and leading the way by providing cheaper drugs that could extend the life of AIDS and HIV sufferers.

And while there was much celebration of the homecoming of whites, *The Sunday Times* was also reporting that "a recruitment firm recently rang alarm bells about the new 'black brain drain.' Nurses and black teachers started to leave from 1999–2000 in search of better pay, and now it is black professionals and managers who are quitting the country at an alarming rate to gain international experience. Whites returning, blacks leaving: a looking-glass South Africa?"

On the last night of February, a development occurred that only history can judge. President Jean-Bertrand Aristide was said to have resigned and was spirited out of Haiti in the dead of night in a plane with its blinds drawn so the ex-president could not determine where he was headed, thereby giving a new meaning to the tragic blinding of a leader in our mythology. Accompanying him were military officials from the United States and France, acting in full knowledge of most Western nations, including Canada. But the leaders of the Black nation-states in the Caribbean that were trying to resolve the Haitian dispute democratically were kept mostly in the dark. And Aristide was expelled to a country that is often called the Haiti of Africa—the Central African Republic, economically and socially the poorest country on the continent, if not in the world.

Perhaps Aristide's ouster was a new beginning, caused by a new revolution. The only certainty was that this was the thirtieth time the Haitian government had been changed by "revolution" since 1804, making the events that closed out Black History Month in 2004 perhaps more a farce than a tragedy. Indeed, the jester must have been snickering, and perhaps people like Froude, Smuts, Wilson, and their Canadian and British Commonwealth counterparts finally felt justified in always pointing to the idol and saying, "Beware! For nothing good ever came out of a Black state." And the final irony in this tragedy was that the country that eventually gave Aristide political asylum was South Africa.

When the southern states revolted against the North in the U.S. and set up their own republican government in the 1860s, the entire world was watching. This was the big showdown on slavery, with the South fighting for the institution's preservation and the North struggling to bring an end to a blight on a union founded on the precepts of liberty, equality, and fraternity. Nowhere was attention more focused on this latest fratricidal war than in the British Empire, where although slavery, if not servitude, had been abolished three decades earlier, there were still some very strongly held positions on the appropriateness of Blacks governing themselves. John Stuart Mill, for example—although arguing in favour of the rights of people to responsible self-government (as developed in Canada), the enfranchisement of women, and the North's principled stance on slavery—did not think it was wise to offer the same liberties and access to representative government to Blacks. Representative government would, however, be offered to white colonies.

But there was another reason for the eyes of the British Empire to watch what was happening in the United States. The implications were severe for the side that won. There was speculation that if the South won, it would not only retain slavery in its states but also annex the Caribbean islands and reintroduce slavery there. If the North won, many in the empire felt, it would be sending the wrong message to those who still remembered the heady days of the Haitian Revolution and dreamed of full democratic citizenship for all humanity in a liberal country. Indeed, this exuberance had already spilled over in Jamaica in 1865, in an event that came to be known as the Morant Bay Rebellion. When a group of mainly *mulattos* staged a revolt to press demands for full citizenship rights, the English governor, John Edward Eyre, panicked and hanged the leader, George William Gordon, for treason. The white elites, sensing that the tide of democracy and liberalism was going against them, voted their legislature out of business and asked Britain to take Jamaica back as a crown colony to be ruled directly from the mother country. At the very moment that white, and primarily English, settlers in Canada were laying the groundwork for a self-governing federation based on the model of representative government, their counterparts in Jamaica, and most of the rest of the Caribbean, were clamouring for direct rule from Westminster. Since because of their numbers they could not become another Canada, they feared becoming another Haiti.

James Anthony Froude saw nothing good in a revolution that gave Blacks full freedom and rule. In his book *The English in the West Indies,* he pointed out that the physical conditions had deteriorated in Haiti from the halcyon days when the capital, Port-au-Prince, was considered the Paris of the Caribbean. "Long before we came ashore," Froude wrote in his introduction to Haiti, "there came off whiffs, not of drains as at Havana, but of active dirt fermenting in sunlight. Calling our handkerchiefs to our help and looking to our feet carefully, we stepped upon the quay and walked forward as judiciously as we could. With the help of stones we crossed a shallow ditch where rotten fish, vegetables, and other articles were lying about promiscuously, and we came on what did duty for a grand parade." This, Froude said, was "a Paris of the gutter, with boulevard and *places, fiacres* and crimson parasols. The boulevards were littered with refuse of the houses and were foul as pigsties, and the ladies under the parasols were picking their way along them in Parisian boots and silk dresses. I saw a *fiacre* broken down in a black pool out of which a blacker ladyship was scrambling. Fever breeds so prodigally in that pestilential squalor that 40,000 people were estimated to have died of it in a single year."[4]

This was the worst of worlds for Blacks and whites alike, in Froude's opinion. The whites he encountered were mere "white trash," unable to own property and insulted on the streets by Black dukes and marquises. Immorality for both Blacks and whites was rampant, and the island suffered from a "horrible revival of the West African superstitions: the serpent worship, and the child sacrifice, and cannibalism." So bad was the situation that "rational and well-disposed Haitians" would have welcomed back the French, but the Americans' Monroe Doctrine would not allow European powers to intervene in the Americas.[5]

The message was quite clear, Froude argued. "One does not grudge the black man his prosperity, his freedom, his opportunities of advancing himself; one would wish to see him as free and prosperous as the fates and his own exertion can make him, with more and more means of raising himself to the white man's level. But left to himself, and without the white man to lead him, he can never reach it." In Froude's estimation, Blacks by nature "are docile, good-tempered, excellent and faithful servants when they are kindly treated; but their notions of right and wrong are scarcely even elementary; their education, such as it may be, is but skin deep, and the old African superstitions lie undisturbed at the bottom of their souls." Taking on the role of the prophet, Froude held out no hope for whites who found themselves under the rule and administration of Blacks—or for the Blacks themselves. Theirs was a hopeless situation that, if left in their hands, could only get worse. "Give them independence," he remonstrated, "and in a few generations they will peel off such civilization as they have learnt as easily and as willingly as their coats and trousers."[6]

The conditions that Froude described were thought by many to occur naturally whenever Blacks were given any level of autonomy—or whenever they lived together as communities in a sea of whiteness. North America had its own "little Haitis" when Froude was writing about the real thing, most notably in Philadelphia and later in Nova Scotia, in what was known as Africville. For the Philadelphia story, we will turn to an influential work by a man who was anticipating a new century that he believed would be marked by a struggle across the colour line. This was the scholar W. E. B. Du Bois and his much-praised book *The Philadelphia Negro: A Social Study,* written in 1899.

"In Philadelphia," Du Bois wrote, "as elsewhere in the United States, the existence of certain peculiar social problems affecting the Negro people are plainly manifest. Here is a large group of people—perhaps forty-five thousand, a city within a city—who do not form an integral part of the larger social group. This in itself is not altogether unusual; there are other unassimilated groups: Jews, Italians, even Americans; and yet in the case of the Negroes the segregation is more conspicuous, more patent to the eye, and so intertwined with a long historic evolution, with peculiarly pressing social problems of poverty, ignorance, crime and labor, that the

Negro problem far surpasses in scientific interest and social gravity most of the other race or class questions."[7]

It's clear that what Du Bois was describing was a common condition for Blacks, or Negroes as they were called then, even in polite society; that there were at the same time other groups that were not as assimilated into the much-vaunted American melting pot; and that Du Bois thought there was a scientific explanation for these social inequities. Du Bois was just a product of his times, but any scientific explanation of social inequality invariably leads into a discussion of race as a supposedly objective way of explaining biological and cultural differences among groups—whether Negroes, Italians, Jews, or even Americans.

Still, we can see in these two works the profound difference between someone like Froude visiting and exploring the Black existence in Haiti and someone like Du Bois visiting and exploring a similar existence in Philadelphia. Froude knew what he was going to find in Haiti even before he stepped off his boat. On the other hand, Du Bois went in search of the answers to specific questions, and supposedly with an open mind. And in trying to grasp what was at stake in a Black colony like Philadelphia's, Du Bois framed questions that we should also be asking as we try to understand this problem of unequal existences that are presented as the natural way of living for a specific group.

"The student of these questions must first ask, What is the real condition of this group of human beings? Of whom is it composed, what sub-groups and classes exist, what sort of individuals are being considered?" Du Bois wrote. "Further, the student must clearly recognize that a complete study must not confine itself to the group, but must specially notice the environment; the physical environment of the city, sections and houses, the far mightier social environment—the surrounding world of custom, wish, whim, and thought which envelops this group and powerfully influences its social development."[8]

In Philadelphia, Du Bois painted a picture of a group of people struggling for decades to improve their lot but being held back by the "social" environment, customs, violence, and even the whims of a "stronger race," as whites were described by another writer in the introduction to the book.[9] None could escape the one-name-fits-all category of "Negro" and later "Black", and even though there were different social classes within this enclave, when its members went beyond their boundaries, all became part of the singular and supposedly inferior class or race of people known as Negroes. This was not the case for the other groups Du Bois mentioned, however. Their members could improve their economic and social status, and eventually be assimilated into the mainstream. Blacks, as a homogenized group, could not.

Du Bois was showing that race is really about how people are socially constructed, how they are placed within or outside the state, and what positions they are allowed to aspire to and achieve within the nation-state. The crimes and dreams, despair and hope—and everything else in between—are determined by social more than physical conditions. In this respect, there is nothing natural about how Blacks "evolved" through history. Rather, history has shaped or constructed them. The notion of the Negro, and its many derivatives (including the coon, as we shall see), was socially constructed. Race begins as a thought in the head, and out of that thought comes the ordering or social construction of society to conform to predetermined ideals and idols. This is when what was merely a thought becomes concrete, a brute fact of a specific kind of lived experience. Even the physical terrain would then reflect the expectations of a specific race of beings living in their "natural" geographic conditions. The suggestion that there was a social explanation for race was not the way Froude saw the so-called Black and African question.

FROUDE WOULD COME to be identified with two other notions that were crucial to the development of the Americas: that Blacks, as a presumed race, were inferior and should (if they were to receive some semblance of civilization) be ruled despotically by whites, and that Haiti typified the worst of what could happen to the world if Blacks were allowed to rule themselves. The Haitian civilization represented the decay that would be inflicted on the entire world if white, and particularly English, culture did not triumph. The English led Froude's social hierarchy, followed by other whites, then Blacks under colonial rule—such as those in the English-speaking Caribbean—then freed Blacks, like those in Haiti. Haiti, for Froude, was the worst example of what came out of the revolts that were commonly associated with the beginnings of Modernity.

His view found strong support in the white British colonies, especially those that would eventually feel betrayed when Britain, to protect its narrowly defined interests, began to cozy up to the United States and debate the merits of giving responsible governments to its colonies in the perceptually Black worlds of India, Africa, the Caribbean, and Catholic Ireland. Indeed, Froude's social hierarchy would influence Canada's immigration policies even into the latter half of the twentieth century, and he made trips to Australia, the United States, and the Caribbean to reinforce his views. He also had important say in what would become known as the South African question.

In formally establishing the Union of South Africa in 1910, white South Africa had rejected Lord Carnarvon's confederation proposals, based on the 1867 Canadian model, because they created too loose a federation and not a strong enough centralized union. The white elites in South Africa wanted a centralized union that would give them a strong hand when dealing with the majority Blacks in any part of the federation. The main criticism was that the proposed model did not take into account South Africa's peculiar situation—a small minority of English and Dutch settlers surrounded by millions of African natives.

Nevertheless, the South African elites were constantly looking to Canada for inspiration and leadership. Often, judges in South Africa turned to Canadian law for guidance in their rulings, and the two countries maintained a strong bond as British dominions that perceptually shared many of the same problems. Their prime ministers were strong allies at many imperial conferences, when leaders from the white territories and Britain met to discuss the state of the empire and the world. And when the South African constitution was penned in 1909, those drafting it turned to the British North America Act for inspiration. Writing in 1935, in a treatise on constitutional law, W. P. M. Kennedy and H. J. Schlosberg described how much was borrowed from Canada.[10] "Whatever had been useful," they wrote, "whatever worked well in the constitutions of the former colonies, and other countries also, was moulded into the new Union constitution. The fathers of the constitution went to the constitutions of Switzerland and the old South African republics for the provincial council executive committee system. They went to Canada for the wording of many sections of the South Africa Act."[11]

As Kennedy and Schlosberg suggest, what happened in South Africa "though a distinct political advance, was not a great constitutional advance," because it had been tried before in other parts of the British Commonwealth—namely, Canada. The division of the country into smaller territories "was not a very great departure from the Canadian provincial system," they wrote, "nor is there anything in the whole of the South Africa Act that cannot be found in the constitutions of other self-governing Dominions."[12]

Indeed, the similarities between the Canadian and the South African models were soon reinforced by the South African court. Justice Bristowe stated, "The status of provincial councils under the South Africa Act is analogous to that of the Canadian provincial legislation under the British North America Act, 1867. There are no doubt differences between them, of which the most important is that in Canada the provincial legislative powers are throughout exclusive while here they are not. But these differences are of degree rather than of kind."[13] The special relationship between Canada and South Africa was solidly established, to the benefit of the elites in both countries.

H. J. May, in *The South African Constitution,* suggests that there was an even deeper fear for the white federalists. They were concerned that with South Africa's Black-to-white population ratio of five to one, individual white settlements would soon be overrun by the native population. Canada's problem was easier to handle. It simply placed its Natives on reservations and restricted the entry into the country of the "turbulent or unruly element in the uncivilized masses." With the Natives on the reserve, Canada could try to civilize them through residential schools and the like, but it was never possible to control the undesirables and to keep them in their place.

Well into the twentieth century, South Africa and Canada shared the same development model, with each country's officials exchanging insights on how to handle the natives and those excluded from the social contract. South Africa patterned its Natives Act for Blacks on Canada's Indian Acts. Together, the two countries formed alliances within the power circles of the British Empire to prevent it from drifting too quickly towards placing non-whites on the same social and political footing as whites, and officials borrowed ideas from one another on how the two countries could resist Blackness.[14]

Canada and South Africa both attempted to control the flow of Blacks and other visible minority groups to create a white nation-state. South Africa had to deal with regulating Blackness within its national boundaries, and its problem was deemed more severe than Canada's because its Black population was five times that of the white. The non-white population in Canada was deliberately kept at a minuscule level, by contrast, even during periods of intense immigration, when almost all of those let in were white and European.

There was another factor that made the Canadian and South African situations different. In Canada, the Natives steadfastly refused to be assimilated, or to become part of a nation that would assimilate them. They would fight for and gain recognition, even winning the right to territorial sovereignty on their homelands or reserves. Canadian whites could argue with legitimacy that First Nations peoples did not want to be part of the wider Canadian nation-state. They wanted to be separate and apart, to remain truly aboriginal to the white state. This point was brought home, to the international embarrassment of Canada, when the Six Nations Iroquois in Ontario went before the League of Nations in 1922 and charged that Ottawa was planning to invade and colonize a separate and independent country.

Chief Deskaheh, the spokesman for the Six Nations, argued before the league that "the legal situation was entirely different" from the matter of internal jurisdiction that Canada was attempting to portray. He said that "the Six Nations were an independent state, bound to Canada only through treaties made between [our] predecessors and the British Government." And he suggested that "the fact that the British had indeed made what were officially called 'treaties' with the Six Nations lent some colour of credibility to the claim."[15]

Canada would eventually prevail, but only after Britain and her allies were able to have the matter deemed an internal dispute that was beyond the jurisdiction of the League of Nations. Still, Canada had suffered much international embarrassment, and the controversy did resonate beyond the country's borders. From early in the dispute, Blacks and "natives" in South Africa, especially those for whom the African National Congress and its allies spoke, adopted a different position. They began to demand full inclusion and full citizenship for all peoples within the geographical boundaries of South Africa. They would not accept non-white states in South Africa, as First Nations had done in North America. They wanted a democratic and inclusive South Africa, where all citizens were equal regardless of their race or cultural background.

The different approach of First Nations groups in Canada and integrationist groups like the ANC was partly why South Africa turned to more stringent measures to achieve its goal. Indeed, the report that set out the case for apartheid argued that a strict, legalistic separation based on race and culture was necessary to prevent the assimilation of whites by Blacks. In Canada, by contrast, the First Nations were unwittingly complicit in the segregationist policy, for once they'd achieved some independence, Canada quickly put them in a colonial relationship and removed virtually all sovereign powers from them.

South Africa would eventually set up a similar system of Bantu homelands, which were supposedly independent countries. In all respects, these were intended to be nations for and by coons. But none of these was recognized as independent by any foreign country. South Africa would eventually try to banish Blacks to these homelands and require them to show passbooks when they re-entered white territories. In a sense, it was an attempt to set up the independent nations that aboriginal populations claimed to have had at the founding of Canada. Like Canada, South Africa argued that its Bantu homeland policy was strictly an internal matter. This time, the international community disagreed.

According to May, in deciding to toughen its stance on the race question and become a republic, South Africa assumed that it could count on Canada to support its hard-line position, something it knew it could not expect from the United States, given its cultural sensitivities and "racial" mixing of people. Even as it was moving towards apartheid, South Africa expected international condemnation. But it also knew its allies. May shows that the initial supporters of apartheid wanted South Africa to remain within the Commonwealth among like-minded friends. Many countries were prepared to back South Africa if other nation-states condemned it for its racial policies.

Opposition was expected from the United States, which, as the supporters of apartheid said, viewed itself as the protector of Western democracies and therefore was unlikely to support racial discrimination. (As we shall see in the next chapter, the elites in Canada held similar views on the U.S. and how its sizeable Black population would shape its world-view and make it anti-racist.) Indeed, May writes, the supporters of apartheid assumed that "only Britain, Australia, Canada, and New Zealand would stand solidly with South Africa. Therefore South Africa should not be a republic, but if she desires to be one, she should remain in the Commonwealth. A great many Afrikaners share this view."[16] History, however, did not play out as the supporters of apartheid expected.

Despite being South Africa's closest friend in the British Empire and nascent Commonwealth, Canada did not stand with the country when it was brought before the United Nations by India to protest the mistreatment of Indian-born South Africans. Indeed, Canada took a stance against apartheid internationally both to save face and to counter criticism from the Soviet Union, and South Africa, too, about its own treatment of its Native populations. Until that happened, the Canadian elites had been prepared to act as peace brokers, trying to get South Africa to tone down some of its more flagrant legalized abuses. A radical change in attitude and support for South Africa occurred in Canada beginning in the 1960s. And in the 1980s, ironically, it was Prime Minister Brian Mulroney who broke ranks with Margaret Thatcher and Ronald Reagan and called for total sanctions against the apartheid regime, a move that led to the eventual collapse of that system. The United States, which apartheid supporters had expected to rail against them, stood beside South Africa to the bitter end. Once again, the South African government felt betrayed by a friend who should have understood its plight.

The scholar Alan C. Cairns explains, in his book *Citizen Plus: Aboriginal People and the Canadian State,* that in the end Canada and South Africa were affected by the same global pressures on human rights for their native populations. "Canadian policy, as it was carried in the mentalities of those who devised and administered it, and more vaguely as was experienced by those who were on the receiving end, rose and fell as a side eddy of global trends in, first, the rise and, subsequently, the demise of [the British] Empire. The latter not only transformed the international system, but also eroded the justification for viewing indigenous peoples at home as subject peoples. From Canada came these two examples: When John Diefenbaker extended the franchise to Status Indians in 1960, the desire to forestall criticism from the leaders of an increasingly multiracial commonwealth, and at the United Nations, was at least as important as placating the Indian peoples, many of whom were suspicious of the suffrage gift. Furthermore, one of the stands that led to the 1969 White Paper proposing to abolish separate Indian status was the desire to overcome Canada's credibility gap at the UN over its Indian policy."[17]

The policy of embarrassing Canada internationally was also used by activist Blacks fighting for recognition and for a reversal of the country's anti-Black immigration policies. In *My Name's Not George: The Story of the Brotherhood of Sleeping Car Porters in Canada,* Stanley Grizzle writes of a brief he presented to Canada's immigration minister, Walter Harris, in Ottawa in 1954. "I called on the Canadian government, in the interest of national and international welfare and security, to immediately remove its 'Jim Crow Iron Curtain' which existed in the country's immigration policy. That curtain affected Canada's ability to win friends and allies among the free nations of the world so long as Canada continued to discriminate against these people."[18]

Faced with mounting global pressure, the South African elites felt they had to reinforce the model developed in Canada. Believing that the Canadian provincial system simply maintained white ethnic jealousies, they decided to limit the powers of the states to make them look less like Canadian provinces. Obviously, the elites did not want to open the door to the possibility of a state declaring itself Black, thereby creating a situation like the one that existed in Canada between the French-speaking province of Quebec and the rest of the country, or even repeating the polarization among the states that led to the American Civil War. The elites also wanted a freer hand to deal with internal problems without having to get approval from Britain, and they were anxious to extend their sovereign powers within the British Commonwealth. At the end of the First World War, Canada would take the lead, asserting itself as a dominion, and South Africa would quickly follow this route. But once again, because of its internal dynamics of race, South Africa had to go one step further than Canada. It became a republic.

Canada's approach, on the other hand, was to work within existing traditions. Specifically, it came to rely on the passport to keep the country white. For almost a hundred years following Confederation, Canada virtually closed its doors to non-white immigration. This was most noticeable in the 1940s, when Blacks from the southern United States began to move north in one of the largest migrations within North America. Although they reshaped the northern United States culturally and demographically, very few of them were allowed to cross the border into Canada. Blacks from the Caribbean and Africa were similarly excluded. Put simply, Canada's immigration policy was aimed at keeping Blacks on their homelands outside of Canada while encouraging whites from Europe to come to a homeland of their own within Canada.

Unlike South Africa, Canada made sure that its Black problem remained external or suppressed. It was a policy that led directly to the human tragedy of Africville in Nova Scotia, the 1960s equivalent in many respects to the turn-of-the-century Philadelphia of Du Bois's work. Africville is more than just the story of how the most vibrant Black and African settlement in Canadian history was erased as an act of government policy. It shows how, in the absence of the questions suggested by Du Bois, prejudice demanded the eradication of a community that the dominant imagination saw as only a slum or a blight on an otherwise pristine landscape. It is also the story of why, in a moment of sober afterthought, Africville was made a National Historic Site by the same federal government that was privy to the original provincial act of erasure. However, it is worth noting that more than a generation had passed before the apology was offered.

THESE, THEN, were some of the historical conditions produced by race within countries intended as white homelands. But there could be no harmony within the world order, or the segment of it that was called the British Empire. Finally, the issue had to come to a head in a battle of visions of nation-state formation. On one side, those like the South African apartheid leader Smuts argued that the world order could consist of part free and part slave, part equal and part unequal, part fully human and part not quite human. This was effectively the position he argued at an imperial conference in London in 1921. On Smuts's side of the debate were his fellow prime ministers from the white British dominions. In the middle was the British prime minister, trying valiantly, but with little success, to keep two warring factions in the same camp. And on the other side was a lone voice, the representative of the Indian prime minister and all Blacks in the British Empire, Sir Tej Sapru. India had asked the conference to denounce South Africa for its treatment of Indians and its refusal to grant them and other non-whites the right to vote. This, the Indian delegations argued, was giving unequal treatment to people who were equal subjects of the British Empire. Smuts and his supporters disagreed. They fell back on the argument Canada was making at the same time to the League of Nations: that the treatment of non-whites was a parochial matter best handled internally by the South African government. It could be of no interest to the wider world. "I tell him [Smuts]," Sir Tej informed the press after the conference, "that if the Indian problem in South Africa is allowed to fester much longer it will become a question of such gravity that on it the unity of the Empire may founder irretrievably."[19]

On that day, Sir Tej was the lone voice, outvoted by members of this club. But on that day, he had become a vassal for the new spirit of the times. And just as Abraham Lincoln and others before him had insisted that no nation-state could survive with one part free and one part slave, he would be proven right. The empire *would* collapse—partially when India and Pakistan became independent in 1947, and then completely when, with one swoop, sixteen former African colonies of the European powers gained their independence in the 1960s and took their places in the United Nations.

In the U.N., this new spirit would be felt. In 1946, the Indian government had asked that the question of apartheid in South Africa be placed on the U.N.'s agenda. Two years later, in July 1948, the Indian delegation again complained about South Africa and warned: "If the belief that there is to be one standard of treatment for the White races and another for the non-White continues to gain strength among the latter, the future for solidarity among the Members of the United Nations and, consequently, for world peace will indeed be dark."[20] South Africa was expelled from the British Commonwealth in 1961, and soon after the United Nations imposed economic sanctions on the only homeland that was officially still wedded to the old model of providing a refuge for whites only.

But by the time of the expulsion, a revolution had taken place elsewhere. Canada, the erstwhile big sister to South Africa and one of the original prototypes of Modernity's nation-state, was once again the voice and embodiment of the new times. It had begun the fight to dismantle the remaining exclusively white homelands worldwide. And in doing this, it had become the very opposite to what its founders had intended. Eventually, Canada would become as Black, symbolically, as Sir Tej Sapru, and as triumphant as the Haitian model of nation-state formation.

By then, Sir Tej had passed the torch of history to another—Prime Minister John Diefenbaker, who would lead the fight to have South Africa expelled from the British Commonwealth and ostracized internationally. Two decades later, another Canadian prime minister, Brian Mulroney, would become the embodiment of the new liberating spirit, staring down his ideological colleagues, Margaret Thatcher and Ronald Reagan, to demand that South Africa be treated as an international outlaw. Mulroney would lead the fight against apartheid in the British Commonwealth and in the United Nations. The result, ultimately, was the election of a multiracial and multi-ethnic government under Nelson Mandela.

Senator Donald Oliver, ironically one of only two Black senators in Canada's history, told a Senate committee what he had witnessed in 1994 as a United Nations observer of the South African elections. "We all realize that, as long as history is written about our world and the triumph of democracy, this election in South Africa will be a major focal point," he said. "It is different because millions of black people stood for hours in lines stretched as far as the eye could see, hour after hour, with little or nothing to eat or drink, in order to have an opportunity to mark their ballots. These Africans had faith in a process which they barely understood; faith that, in the end, the will of the people—democracy—would prevail. Their faith was rewarded—a black man, a former political prisoner, is now president, leading his own black people's party." Modernity's revolution had come full circle. In spirit, the entire world was now Haitian.

chapter three

MOUNTAINTOPS, VALLEYS,
AND MULTICULTURALISM

"Once upon a time," recounted Jan Christiaan Smuts in 1923 to a select group of citizens assembled on the famous Table Mountain, which gives the Cape Town area of his native South Africa one of its distinctive characteristics, "in the far-off beginning of things, the ancestors of the present human race lived far down in deep blue pools of the ocean, amid the slimy ooze from which they had sprung. There they lived and developed a long time, and in the sounds of the sea, in the rhythm of the waters, and of the rising and falling tides, they learnt that sense of music which is so mysterious a faculty in us, and which is in a much smaller degree shared by so many marine animals."[1] There was something special about our ancestors, the statesman, military hero, and builder of venerable international institutions recalled. They found that the pressures of the water were too much a hindrance for them. They felt stifled and longed for freedom. They crawled ashore, and unlike other animals on the land, even those with wings, they kept reaching for higher heights.

On that mountainside, Smuts looked back to the beginning of time and then forward to the end of time. What happened in between was a story of progress and of human upliftment and achievement. This is the story of good and evil, and of the human inclination to do what is naturally good. This is the story of humans striving to achieve their potential, and of discerning which environment is best suited to that endeavour. This is the story of race and its promissory note to us, and of how, fortunately, the amount paid was always more than expected.

"And so it has come about that finally in man all moral and spiritual values are expressed in terms of altitude," said Smuts. "The low expresses degradation, both physical and moral. If we wish to express great intellectual or moral or spiritual attainments we use the language of the altitudes. We speak of men who have risen, of aims and ideals that are lofty, we place the seat of our highest religious ideals in high heaven, and we consign all that is morally base to nethermost hell. Thus the metaphors embedded in language reflect but the realities of the progress of terrestrial life."

Smuts was, at different times, a field marshal, the prime minister of the Union of South Africa, a dreamer of a perpetual world peace based on equality of all men and women, and one of the founding fathers of apartheid, the official policy of separating peoples according to their perceived races. He was the embodiment of a special spirit of his times. But it was an indeterminate spirit, like a source that issues forth both bitter and sweet, like a being that is at once good and evil. And there was no way of explaining why these contradictions existed. This spirit looked to uplift humanity, but at the same time, paradoxically, it offered that uplifting to only a small segment of humanity. Smuts embodied the hope and despair that—like certainty and doubt—are the twins of human existence.

His intention was to create good for humanity. He was a leading figure in the formation of the League of Nations after the First World War. When that failed, he was among the first to scoop from the ashes the foundations of what would become the United

Nations. This phoenix-like institution is now purportedly the holy temple of world morality, a place where the nations of the world gather not so much to express their differences but to foster the good ethical relations that will prevent them, in acts of national pride and selfishness, from destroying themselves. The United Nations is itself a contradiction—a world body that practises globalism through the exercise of a singular nationalism. This singular nationalism is based on the idea that although the different "nations" of the world operate in their specific and often narrow interests, they nevertheless end up working together for the betterment and preservation of humanity in general. Its main aim is to help humanity work through—and live with—its own contradictions, without resorting to destruction.

Smuts, as president of the Commission on the General Assembly, drafted the preamble of the United Nations' charter. The charter came into force on October 24, 1945. From all indications, Smuts was sincere and intended only good. He knew what visions could be seen from the highest places. "The Mountain is not merely externally sublime. It has a great historic and spiritual meaning for us. It stands for us as the ladder of life," he said in his Table Mountain speech. "Nay, more it is the great ladder of the soul, and in a curious way the source of religion. From it came the Law, from it came the Gospel in the Sermon on the Mount. We may truly say that the highest religion is the Religion of the Mountain."

Smuts had gone to the summit of Table Mountain, which overlooks the city of Cape Town, to tell his story of humanity's achievements and its desires. He unveiled a war memorial at the top of the mountain—which stands 1,086 metres (3,563 feet) high and gives clear views in every direction—in a place called Maclear's Beacon. This was a memorial for those who'd died in the Great War, which only four years earlier had been devastating Europe. Like Abraham Lincoln had done in 1863 at the Gettysburg cemetery, Smuts was consecrating a place that he hoped future generations would view as hallowed ground, where they would recall with honour the sacrifices and achievements of those who'd died to secure the advancement of their society. But there was a significant difference between Lincoln and Smuts. One wanted his land to become a place of inclusion, while the other wanted his to exclude the majority of humanity. This was where the Haitian model of the Modern state would prove unworthy only for those of lesser ability, culture, and status. And because they were of an inferior pedigree, they would be reminded that this was a place where they did not belong. They would not be capable of achieving great heights. Practitioners of the Haitian model of human integration would be excluded.

The white homeland Smuts advocated, like the marker at the top of the mountain, would be a monument to freedom and the triumph of human hope. It would be testament to the highest achievement of the human spirit: the nation-state. It would withstand the ravages of time, making those whose memory it stood for as immortal as gods. They would have conquered the death of a decaying memory and slipped the bonds of humanity and the decomposition of body and spirit that is the human condition.

But Smuts could not see his own contradictions. He did not understand that although he was telling a story about the universal beginnings of humanity, he was using it as the basis for an ordered separation of a unified human race into an ordered hierarchy of races and nations, with the superior ones at the top and the inferior ones at the bottom. In his view, the solidarity and fraternity enjoyed at the beginning of history had to be left behind at the end of history. The brotherhood of humanity had to be left in the primordial muck from which perfected humans had emerged. Smuts argued that the laws of evolution were clear. And the fulfillment of those laws, which was the spirit of Modernity, meant bringing unchallenged certainty where there used to be doubts. This was religion taking the form of a secular ideology, one that falsely promised that a minority could advance if the majority were held back. Smuts was preaching a morality built on the belief that a special minority was better than an ordinary majority, and that both groups on either side of that natural divide could fulfil their natural destiny only by living apart in nation-states of their own.

On the African continent, this destiny was found in a new national spirit that was South Africa, a place that was to be a garden of European civilization and culture in the purported wilds that were the rest of Africa. According to Smuts, South Africa was to be a white man's country. It would become the symbol of all that is good, a monument to white purity and to the technological and scientific advancement that supposedly underpinned it. South Africa, Smuts said, would be a refuge for Europeans then enduring "the Ten Plagues" of war, the worst of the human condition. South Africa would preserve and maintain what was considered the best of European civilization. Apartheid South Africa would be the Augustinian city on the hill, a shining example to others, especially all those countries that started as European settler colonies. South Africa would be a place built on race—a place that symbolized how some people became like gods, or at least lived and acted that way.

According to this thinking, in their hands would rest the blue-prints for the most perfect and civil humans. To this end, the world would be divided into two clear races: one that was white-skinned and almost as perfect as gods; the other non-white and failing to escape its primordial humanity. According to this view, it was not natural for gods to live among humans, and it was far less natural for them to be ruled by mere men and women.

"We have started by creating a new white base in South Africa," Smuts said in another speech, "and today we are in a position to have moved forward towards the North and the civil-isation of the African Continent. Our problem is a very difficult one, however; quite unique in its way. In the United States there is a similar problem of black and white with the Negro population. But there you have had an overwhelming white population with a smaller Negro element in the midst of it. In South Africa the situation is reversed. There you have an overwhelming black population with a small white population which has got a footing there and which has been trying to make the footing secure for more than two centuries." If it was successful, Smuts believed, South Africa would be more united than the United States of America, with its Negro question, and "Canada, where French-Canadians are also standing aside from the general current of Canadian life and national development." Unity, for Smuts, would come through separation and the segregation of each perceived race. It would come through the very opposite of what he promoted for good world order. In place of the inclusiveness that he argued for in the preamble to the U.N. charter, he posited the exclusivity of a single group for South Africa. The laws of this religion were clear. "With us there are certain axioms now in regard to the relations of white and black; and the principal one is 'no intermixture of blood between the two colours.' It is probably true that earlier civilisations have largely failed because that principle was never recognized, civilising races being rapidly submerged in the quicksands of African blood. It has now become an accepted axiom in our dealings with the natives that it is dishonourable to mix white and black blood."

As the political scientist James Barber reported in his book *South Africa's Foreign Policy: The Search for Status and Security, 1945–1988,* "For him [Smuts] the overriding task in international affairs was to prevent a third world war, and to achieve this he supported three major objectives: first, the creation of an international organization designed to preserve the peace; second, the restoration of a peaceful and prosperous Europe; and third, the reinforcement and expansion of the British Commonwealth of Nations. These objectives, as seen by Smuts, were not mutually exclusive but knitted together to reinforce each other." This was more the man and dreamer who'd insisted that the U.N. charter should commit the world body "to re-establish faith in fundamental human rights, in the sanctity and ultimate value of human personality, in the equal rights of men and women." These words were changed to say that the body "reaffirms faith in fundamental human rights, in the dignity and worth of the human person, in the equal rights of men and women," but the thoughts and the spirit were still Smuts's.

Certain that he had discovered the laws of human excellence that Modernity had promised, Smuts descended from the summit of the mountain into the planes of human activity, leaving history to discern the truth and destiny of humanity, and to pass judgment on him. In the valley below, he would be concerned with the day-to-day affairs of building a nation-state and of capturing a specific spirit. In this descent, Smuts himself would be transfigured: he would become an archetype of the tragic figure of Modernity. Over time, he would come to symbolize its worst evils: the dashed hopes of those seeking to become fully human, in solidarity with all other members of humanity. Smuts, like the white apartheid state that he helped found, became an international symbol of evil, the very opposite of the goodness that even he had intended for all human-ity. Smuts and his ilk became morally hollow men, without souls and humanity. They were shunned and ostracized, denounced as evil incarnate and as followers of rules that ran counter to the hopes and aspirations of the brotherhood and sisterhood of all humanity.

Good intentions had, in the judgment of history, produced evil outcomes. The jester was snickering again. Smuts had become immoral by espousing an ideology or religion that could not address its own internal contradictions. And because it could not, all that was done in the name of this ideology could only be ethi-cally bad. In the end, the Europe that Smuts had hoped to revive turned its back on his handmaiden, the Union of South Africa. The British Commonwealth rejected the union's membership. And although the United Nations had helped the world to avoid that dreaded third world war, it had also repudiated the parochial idea of the man who gave the world body its charter and defined its holistic spirit. "Ironically," wrote Barber, "these very words [of equality in the U.N.'s charter] would soon be turned against him and his country as a new idealism, the search for equality between black and white, was taken up."

Smuts embodied the contradictions of living and knowing what is true and right. And in the end, he was sacrificed on the very gallows that he had built. His was a story of an unhappy consciousness, of the human failure to see that universalism and goodwill are necessary for the building of national and international unions of perpetual peace. Smuts's downfall, and South Africa's, came because he convinced himself that human beings could be divided, instead of accepting, as he surely knew and had even forced the world to acknowledge, that humanity is genuinely indivisible. Race equals divisions. Evil, therefore, is the destruction of human solidarity and raceless indeterminacy.

But as if to prove that the jester was indeed at work, Smuts and his followers did give some good to the world. Unintentionally, they gave us three of the greatest men of Modernity: Mahatma Gandhi, who developed his ideology of peaceful resistance in South Africa and went on to lead India to independence when the British Empire collapsed and became the commonwealth of nations that Smuts had always envisioned; Martin Luther King, Jr., who borrowed from Gandhi the intellectual armour of peaceful resistance that helped dismantle segregation in the United States and brought an excluded people fully into America's Modernity; and Nelson Mandela, who began his rise to international fame and the presidency of the Union of South Africa in a struggle with Smuts himself. These men were all of one spirit, and that same spirit can still be found at the top of Table Mountain, which now looks down on an officially multicultural Cape Town below. But today that spirit is found not in a monument to the past glories of great men long since forgotten, but in a world-famous restaurant that feeds all those—tourists and South African nationals alike—who have struggled to arrive at that great height and, once there, seek nourishment in the breaking of bread before beginning the hard work of descending once more to the lived world below.

FOUR DECADES AFTER Smuts's own descent from the summit of Table Mountain, another statesman reported on his view from a mountaintop. "Well, I don't know what will happen now. We've got some difficult days ahead," said Martin Luther King, Jr., on the night before he was assassinated in 1968. "But it doesn't matter with me now. Because I've been to the mountaintop. And I don't mind. Like anybody, I would like to live a long life. Longevity has its place. But I'm not concerned about that now. I just want to do God's will. And He's allowed me to go up to the mountain. And I've looked over. And I've seen the promised land. I may not get there with you. But I want you to know tonight, that we, as a people, will get to the promised land. And I'm happy tonight. I'm not worried about anything. I'm not fearing any man. Mine eyes have seen the glory of the coming of the Lord."

Five years earlier, in his "I Have a Dream" speech at the Lincoln Memorial, King had offered an even more explicit report of what he had seen. He'd invoked the legacy of Abraham Lincoln and his Gettysburg address, reminding us of the days when the young nation had flagellated itself over the issue of slavery and whether it could for long continue as half free and half slave. For these are the uncertainties endemic to the human condition, where good never appears without evil and even in evil there is some good. In his own address, King noted that one hundred years after the Civil War, fought to settle the issue that supposedly went to the heart of the survival of the nation-state, "the life of the Negro is still sadly crippled by the manacles of segregation and the chains of discrimination." American Blacks remained outside the nation-state that was the United States, even if they had a physical presence within the country. This was an evil that still existed, even though Lincoln and others had spilled blood for a different ending. African-Americans had not yet been brought into Modernity through its proudest achievement, the nation-state. This was a promissory note that still had to be redeemed, although it might have become devalued in the meantime.

In the words of King, "This note was a promise that all men … would be guaranteed the unalienable rights of life, liberty, and the pursuit of happiness. It is obvious today that America has defaulted on this promissory note insofar as her citizens of color are concerned. Instead of honoring this sacred obligation, America has given the Negro people a bad check, a check which has come back marked 'insufficient funds.' But we refuse to believe that the bank of justice is bankrupt. We refuse to believe that there are insufficient funds in the great vaults of opportunity of this nation." And without saying it explicitly, King and his followers were also refusing to accept that the fraternity and solidarity for all peoples, as promised by Modernity and captured in the spirit of the Haitian Revolution, would not come to fruition. They believed that their hopes, fears, and despairs could still be reconciled under the prevailing ideology, and that they could explain rationally the contradictions that left one part of their nation-state free and the other enslaved by keeping their fellow citizens in bondage. King was not talking about people who had ascended the ladder to become like gods; his people were still cast down among the poor. They were still being held in human bondage. They still knew only death and the promise, someday, of everlasting life.

But even before that day arrived, humanity had to take the first step to full status before continuing the journey to supposedly absolute perfection that is at the summit of human aspirations. Society first had to prove that it could not only explain away its ideological contradictions but even make good all that is evil. King and his followers were refusing to remain in a deficit position, unfulfilled and alienated from their dreams and desires. "I have a dream that one day ... little black boys and black girls will be able to join hands with little white boys and white girls as sisters and brothers," said King. "I have a dream today. I have a dream that one day every valley shall be exalted, and every hill and mountain shall be made low; the rough places will be made plain, and the crooked places will be made straight; and the glory of the Lord shall be revealed, and all flesh shall see it together. This is our hope. This is the faith.... With this faith we will be able to hew out of the mountain of despair a stone of hope. With this faith we will be able to transform the jangling discords of our nation into a beautiful symphony of brotherhood. With this faith we will be able to work together, to pray together, to struggle together, to go to jail together, to stand up for freedom together, knowing that we will be free one day."

The approaches of Smuts and King could not have been more different. One wanted segregation and apartheid, the other solidarity and fraternity. Smuts invoked a religion of certainty based on known laws, axioms, and specific outcomes. Under these laws, there were no contradictions and evil was always known and boxed in. King, on the other hand, offered hope and faith in a world of uncertainty and acknowledged injustices. In his world, people often acted in good faith but failed to deliver as expected, and in the end, they appeared as evil and unjust as they would have if they had intentionally desired such outcomes. Smuts looked to the day when his people would be living like gods at the summits of the world. King agonized over a death that was always stalking, and he warned that a poverty of spirit can make us soldiers in the army of death. He appealed to a morality that is predicated on the oneness of humanity, and he preached that the advancement and fulfillment of humanity's progress would come to the many and not the few. Smuts wanted a memorial to history, to all that had been achieved so far, for his future promised little more than a repeat of the past. King was looking to the future, to a new beginning of sorts, and he wanted a clear break, similar to the one Smuts had talked of when our ancestors crawled out of the primordial swamp. Yet in looking for that break with the past, he knew that the settling of old debts could also shape the future, just as debts that are deliberately left outstanding can poison future relations. Standing figuratively on the mountaintop of Modernity, looking down on the people and the nation-states they formed, Smuts and King saw different things. Ironically, though, both men saw the same kind of evil—the "quicksand" (they used the same word) of history, immorality, and poor ethical relations against which they both laboured. In the end, their main difference was one of perspective. And the view they took shaped what they saw.

Smuts would often invoke the image of the Greek god Prometheus, who gave humans fire so that they would become civilized. But in stealing fire from his fellow gods, Prometheus provoked their ire. As punishment, they tied him to the side of a mountain. With time, Prometheus and the mountain rocks would fuse together, thereby becoming, in this version of the myth, the embodiment and symbol of a new and civilized human spirit. This was the same kind of spirit Smuts wanted to develop in an all-white South Africa. "Here," he said, speaking of the mountaintop, "for a thousand years their memory [the war dead] shall blend with the great rock masses and humanise them. The men and women of the coming centuries, who will in ever-increasing numbers seek health and inspiration on this great mountain summit, will find here not only the spirit of Nature, but also the spirit of man blending with it, the spirit of joy in Nature deepened and intensified by the memory of the great sacrifice here recorded." And here we see another contradiction in Smuts, for in invoking the image of Prometheus, he was telling only one part of the story.

The part he favoured had Prometheus elevating humans from their lowly status of living from one season to another like bees or ants to the level of gods who have escaped the hold of time. What he neglected to mention was that in the end, even Prometheus, a god, wanted to become human. Even this god wanted an end of history, a new beginning, and an in-between time that would allow him to change, to move from one status or being to becoming what he thought was more desirable. In Smuts, we see the reversal of the Prometheus myth: a human playing at being a god. Humans, as both Prometheus and Smuts realized, must by nature know death as part of life. The human act is to make death and dying useful, as Prometheus wished, as the price for some greater gain. This was the part of the myth that resonated in King's version of humanity's quest for freedom—a freedom in which people would no longer fear death, a freedom in which they would always be changing without ever fully developing as an ideal.

For King, the mountaintop was also the battlefield, a place for bringing disparate peoples and groups together. Symbolically, this was the site for the realization of the long-held dream in human mythology of uniting the peoples of the world as one in a Tower of Babel, the pinnacle of all humanity and its achievements. As it was in the Bible, humanity would be fully reconciled at last, and all contradictions would be answered. At the same time, humanity's inherent and necessary differences would be recognized, for the human race is diverse, and the beauty of this place is in the disparate tongues and cultures that come from people scattered across the face of the earth.

Yet there is equality in being part of a single race, with all members gathered at the summit of this achievement and the Tower of Babel gleaming proudly in all its multiculturalism. "This will be the day," King said, "when all of God's children will be able to sing with a new meaning, 'My country, 'tis of thee, sweet land of liberty, of thee I sing. Land where my fathers died, land of the pilgrim's pride, from every mountainside, let freedom ring!' ... When we let [freedom] ring from every village and every hamlet, from every state and every city, we will be able to speed up that day when all of God's children, black men and white men, Jews and Gentiles, Protestants and Catholics, will be able to join hands and sing in the words of the old Negro spiritual, 'Free at last! Free at last. Thank God Almighty, we are free at last!'"

In seeking to uplift all parts of humanity, King was simply trying to bring all people to the mountaintop, the place where race no longer matters but people, even in their differences, do. Yes, he was acknowledging contradictions that are inherent to ethical relations in any society, and he was trying to resolve these contradictions within the prevailing social ethos and according to the rules of a commonly held ideology. Even with King, however, the jester seemed to be at play, allowing ambiguity and indeterminacy to rule. For when King spoke of "we as a people," he used the same language as Smuts and appeared to be asking us to think of Blacks as a specific and unique racialized group. Or was he thinking of "we, the people" as all the members of the nation-state? Can one group enter the promised land without the others? This is the knot of race that binds us so ambiguously to the rocks.

BEFORE SMUTS AND KING, others had been to Modernity's mountaintop and had caught its spirit, for good or evil. Each opposing group in North America during the American Revolution, the first attempt at Modernity's nation-state creation, had its spokesmen and visionaries, each claimed to be the proud heir of Modernity's legacy, and each knew the laws and axioms of good and evil.

In Canada, John G. Simcoe, the first lieutenant-governor of Upper Canada, led the way. Devoutly loyal to the English monarchy, he had been commander of the Queen's Rangers, the light cavalry regiment that was among the last to surrender to the victorious Americans. After the revolution, Simcoe returned to England, where he plotted the demise of the experiment that had produced the United States of America. He could not accept that the revolutionaries of the Thirteen Colonies really knew what they wanted; he did not believe they understood the ramifications of seeking democratic, as opposed to aristocratic, rule—of choosing republicanism over the monarchy. He decided he would put a stop to their misguided imaginings, which, like a Greek tragedy, had been caused by the gods putting false dreams in the heads of the people.

What he could not achieve by force of arms, he would by demonstration and reason, for Simcoe fervently believed that most Americans were eager to return to British rule. As John Dafoe says in *Canada: An American Nation*, "The outcome of the Revolution and the establishment of the Republic was to him [Simcoe] some kind of horrid dream that would pass away. He hoped that the establishment of a model government, new colonial style, in the forest of Upper Canada would in some way contribute to this end." In his own papers, Simcoe sketched out a plan and a purpose for Canada and for history. The country would stand in opposition to the United States of America. "I mean to prepare," Simcoe wrote, "for whatever Convulsion may happen in the United States and the Method I propose is by establishing a free honorable British Government and a pure administration of its Laws which shall hold out to the solitary Emigrant, and to the several States, advantages that the present form of government doth not and cannot permit them to enjoy. There are inherent Defects in the Congressional form of government; the absolute prohibition of an order of nobility is one."[2]

One more thing is notable about Simcoe. In 1796, he attempted to abolish slavery in Canada, precipitating one of the first crises between the colonies and the mother country. If he had been successful, he would have made Canada the first colony in the

British Empire to abolish slavery, well ahead of the Americans, who as a nation-state still had to fight a civil war over the issue. Indeed, Simcoe was philosophically in solidarity with the revolutionaries who were then just beginning their struggle in Haiti—a struggle whose aims were the abolition of slavery and the establishment of Modernity's first Black republic of free men and women. He was also following the path set by Vermont, which in 1777 had become the first American colony to abolish the peculiar institution of slavery.[3]

But Simcoe's move was seen as too visionary and too disruptive to the institutions on which European civilized society was founded.[4] The British Privy Council, ironically siding symbolically and philosophically with the slaveowners in the United States rather than with the slave liberators in Haiti, ruled that Simcoe was acting illegally and struck down his abolition bill. Canada, like the rest of the British Empire, would have to wait until 1838 for slavery to be officially abolished. However, Britain handed Simcoe a partial victory by agreeing that any escaped slaves who reached Canada would be free. This paved the way for the creation of the Underground Railroad, which allowed slaves in the United States to escape to freedom in Canada, and it led to the erasure notion in popular history that slavery was never part of the Canadian experience. Simcoe's Canada was intended to be Modernity's alternative to the United States, both spiritually and temporally.

The historian W. L. Morton notes, in his book *The Canadian Identity*, that the creation of Canada was quite deliberate, and that the clearly articulated aim was to provide a reaction to what was happening in the United States. The British possessions in North America would compete against, and even defeat in the game of nation building, the former British possessions that were now the United States of America. Morton argues that Canada was not a historical accident or an artificial creation. There was a specific reason for having a country called Canada in the Americas. "It was an attempt," Morton writes, "to develop in a particular North American environment a civilization European in origin and American in evolution. Certain factors in its history and circumstances give a distinct character to the development and existence of Canada."[5] Thought of this way, Canada was not intentionally much different from South Africa—one was imaginatively a piece of Europe in the Americas; the other was a piece of Europe in Africa. Both were intended as islands of enlightenment and progress in proverbial seas of darkness and primitivism. Both were integral parts of what was seen as the racially white Atlantic when Canada and South Africa were imaginatively tied to Western Europe. This model of Canada was different in one significant way from the one Simcoe had imagined—it was based on race.

That distinctiveness of which Morton wrote remained central to the Canadian identity and character for almost three hundred years, even though the strand of thought was constantly in conflict with the dominant image of Canada as historically European and white. Almost one hundred years after the cataclysmic events of the War of American Independence, which precipitated the creation of Canada, Canadians were taking another step to enshrine their distinctiveness, even as the Americans were fighting a civil war.

But as so often happens in history, the outcome was the opposite of what was intended. The last laugh of the jester would be heard in the 1960s, when Canadians decided that their country would be officially raceless. When they decided to make theirs the world's first officially multicultural country, Canadians were tapping into a vein that had always been part of the Canadian body politic; they were harking back to the universalism and humanity that Lord Simcoe had epitomized. In his day, Simcoe knew Canada was not exclusively European, and he did much to enhance this feature of the Canadian identity. Indeed today, fittingly, we observe Simcoe Day, which marks the abolition of slavery in the British Commonwealth, alongside the largest annual outdoor festival in

Canada, a celebration of the cultural contributions of Caribbeans and Blacks in general. This is the Caribana festival, which started in 1967—Canada's centenary—as an attempt to show how the country has changed, and to give those who were formerly on the outside of Canadian culture a platform. A significant part of the festivities mark the emancipation of slavery and the recognition that Modernity's nation-state cannot exist half free and half slave. Sometimes the circle comes full circle, even if it is broken.

ON APRIL 15, 1783, the War for American Independence finally ended, even though the shooting had long since stopped. A new treaty had come into force between the British Loyalists and the American rebels, setting the two groups on different historical paths—one to withdrawal to French Quebec and English Nova Scotia, the other to start a new republic, the United States of America. There was a third group, a faction of those English men and women who came to North America, and its members returned to the "mother country," where they continued to wage a propaganda and philosophical war against the United States. Eventually, Canada became the theatre for many of the ideas on governance and social order that were put forward by those Loyalists based in London. One of these thinkers, Joseph Galloway, would have a far-reaching impact on the development of British colonialism and on Canada as a colony.[6]

Even before his exile in England, Galloway so badly disagreed with political developments in the Thirteen Colonies that he left political life in Pennsylvania to exile and isolate himself from what was happening. This meant breaking ties with political associates like Benjamin Franklin, one of the founding fathers of the American union. Galloway was a Pennsylvania representative at the First Continental Congress, where Britain's seemingly unfair taxation and trade laws were debated and the developments that would lead to the founding of the United States of America were put in motion. He opposed any break with the mother country and spoke out angrily in defence of this position. "His seclusion was reinforced by his attitude towards Britain—the greatest of nations, the most ideal of governments, the most humane and advanced of monarchies," explained the historian John A. Schutz. "Confirmed in the belief that nothing could be done to improve Britain, he admired its stability, long history, responsible leadership, magnificent constitution; he believed that no person, using his rational senses, would dare overturn this artistic creation of centuries."[7] Even if he misrecognized the spirit, Galloway thought he knew a golden idol when he saw one. He was of the same mindset that would later produce Smuts and others like him, including those in Canada who appeared to be on the same side as Lord Simcoe but disagreed with what he imagined for the nation-states that would develop in the Americas.

But in April 1783, word came that Britain would be strictly abiding by the terms of the peace agreement that had been signed in Paris on November 30, 1782. Now many contradictions arose. Those who'd fought for freedom found themselves enslaved, just like those who'd decided there was no use in fighting. Justice was denied to both groups of people because of one thing: they were deemed to be of an inferior race. Whether they fought against or acquiesced to the slaveowners, there was no place for them in Modernity's civil society. Their choices would not have real meaning for them until the spirit fully manifested itself in Haiti.

But the armistice did allow Loyalists to take their property with them to what would become Canada. Thousands of African slaves planned to join the trek into this wilderness in the hopes of finding a new land that would be theirs by a new covenant. They were the ones who had fought for the Loyalists or escaped into their protection during the war. According to the agreement, all refugees who had been living behind British lines for twelve months were supposedly free to join the exodus. The former slaves felt that included them, for under their perceived covenant with the British they had been made free when they took up arms on the side of the Loyalists. But they were disappointed. When they tried to leave, they were told the agreement did not apply to all of them. Many of the former slaves were still defined by the peace treaty as property, and the new Americans had petitioned to get their property back. Indeed, George Washington, who was responsible for implementing the peace agreement on the American side, was adamant that *all* slaves were property. This was the case, he argued, whether they'd been captured by the British or had come to their side willingly. They should be returned. And so began the series of disappointments Blacks would have with the Loyalists who founded Canada.

The issue of which of the former slaves were entitled to leave was finally settled by a joint British–American board that was set up to examine the merits of every Black application. This board was for Blacks alone and did not concern itself with departing white Loyalists, even those who took all their property with them, including their slaves. In a move that would mirror the emancipation of slaves in British territories in 1834 (when Britain nationalized the slave industry throughout its empire, at a cost of £20 million, and then set the slaves free), the British paid compensation for those who were allowed to leave. Those slaves who were unable to prove they were not someone else's property were returned. The lucky ones were granted a certificate of freedom, which allowed them to go wherever they pleased. Although some went to the Spanish-owned Floridas and to the English-speaking Caribbean, the majority went to Nova Scotia, where the British had promised land, justice, and recognition to all Loyalists.

The symbol of Blackness at the rebirth that would become Canada begins with a refugee camp. A panel of judges, drawing on their own imaginings, would decide whose names would be entered into a new book of life called "Carleton's Book of Negroes," for the

British commander-in-chief, Sir Guy Carleton, who was responsible for protecting British interests under the peace treaty. The refugee board met in a tavern every Wednesday between ten in the morning and two in the afternoon. The historian James Walker writes, "Over the succeeding few weeks Carleton's 'Book of Negroes' was filled in, recording the name, age and description of every black desiring to leave New York, the details of his escape or other claim to freedom, his military record, the name of his former master, and the name, commander and destination of the vessel in which he was removed. Ships' captains were threatened with prosecution for carrying any black not listed on the inspection roll. Masters were then free to challenge any alleged slave and bring him before the board for adjudication. Slaves were permitted to initiate cases before the board if they believed they were being held illegally."[8]

Estimates suggest that 10 percent of the Loyalists who moved to Nova Scotia were Black. But many who thought they were entitled to a fresh beginning found their names not listed in this new book of life. They were returned to slavery, to what the sociologist Orlando Patterson so aptly calls "social death." The old myth—the one that suggested that by fighting for the right cause, they would be rewarded with a new life—did not hold true for them. The promise had been that even if they died, physically or spiritually, they could rest secure in the knowledge of the blessed memories that nation builders as diverse as Plato, Aristotle, Pericles, and an earlier British commander-in-chief, Sir Henry Clinton, had spoken about. Indeed, Clinton had indicated, in his Philipsburg Proclamation of 1779, that "to every NEGRO who shall desert the Rebel Standard, full security to follow within these Lines, any Occupation which he shall think proper."[9]

A legacy of betrayal marked those Haitian Blacks who fought for American independence, many of whom took home to their island the ideal of liberty and justice for all, which became one of the rallying cries of the Haitian Revolution as well. This betrayal would last for centuries, undermining Haiti's development as an independent state. The U.S. did not recognize Haiti until 1862 out of deference to France, and in 1915, the Americans invaded the country and ended the experiment in Black government. As it turned out, the only Blacks who were allowed free and unencumbered passage into Quebec or Nova Scotia were those being taken there by their owners as slaves. Indeed, many of the slaves who were allowed in Canada remained slaves, owned by the rich Loyalists who took whatever moveable property they could to the new land. This was one of the times when the promised new life was in every respect as bitter as the one that was left behind. Those Black slaves who went to Quebec supplanted in numbers the *panis,* First Nations peoples who'd been held in servitude even then.

Segregation was alive and well in Canada, even in its churches, where Blacks were forbidden to mingle with or to sit in the same pews as whites. (In 1784, a special gallery was added to St. Paul's Anglican Church in Halifax for Blacks.) Blacks even had to provide their own clergymen from among their numbers. The fact that Blacks lived under a form of apartheid was noted in 1784 by none other then the Methodist Church founder, John Wesley. "The work of God among the blacks in your neighbourhood is a wonderful instance of the power of God," he wrote, "and the little town they have built is, I suppose, the only town of negroes which has been built in America—nay, perhaps in any part of the world, except in Africa. I doubt not but some of them can read. When, therefore, we send a preacher or two to Nova Scotia, we will send some books to be distributed among them; and they never need want books while I live. It will be well to give them all the assistance you can in every possible way."[10]

It is worth pointing out that Wesley, in all his generosity, meant for only the books to go to the Black communities, not the preachers that his church would be sending out as well. It is also worthy of note that Wesley identified the all-Black community as unheard of in any country other than those in Africa. His observation included all the European-settled countries of the Americas and the Pacific. The same thing was happening in education, where schools in Black communities were built by, staffed, and maintained by Blacks for Blacks. But the result of this educational and religious segregation was that Blacks were living in an apartheid setting, similar to the reservation system of the First Nations peoples and what would eventually happen in South Africa, when the English and the Afrikaners tried to deal with their own "native problem." The result was the creation of parallel, and inferior, social and civic structures for Blacks. Parallel societies that were supposedly "separate but equal" would become the official mark of nation building in the United States well into the 1960s. As James Walker writes, in reference to Canada, "Because they were kept separate these institutions did not lead the blacks into white society. Rather, they encouraged the development of a parallel society: Black, Christian and to some extent educated, different from their white neighbours but different too from the slave culture they left behind."

And here we may recall Wesley's statement that this was a society like no other he knew. Walker concurs. This separation and segregation produced what "was, in fact, *a unique society*, and however much they differed over religion or in their experiences with land and employment, still they belonged to a new way of life that began and grew in Loyalist Nova Scotia"[11] (italics added). This system was unique not only to North America but to the world. Like Prometheus' gift at the beginning of history, this was what Canada gave to the world, to the making of culture, and to the civilizing of humanity. Simcoe's dream of a haven for all humanity, especially the downtrodden political refugee, had been relegated to the dustbin of history by a new stream of Canadian leaders and the elites who supported them.

"SIR WILFRID LAURIER said the 18th century was England's, the 19th belonged to the United States, and that the 20th would be Canada's. Perhaps I am the only being alive who really believes that. For I do—implicitly. I believe that before the year 2000 Canada's world dominance will be as undisputed a fact as any commonplace of history."[12] So opened the book *My Vision of Canada,* published in 1933 and written by William Arthur Deacon, one of the country's foremost intellectuals of the time and the man generally credited with nurturing the body of work that came to be called Canadian literature. This was the base for the cultural institutions developed during the 1950s and 1960s, institutions that would help to mould an image of Canada as a nation that was not British (because of the supposed betrayal by the mother country) and not American (because it was not Black in character, and because the Americans had, unenviably, "all the faults and loveable qualities of irresponsible childhood").[13] This was a Canada that was, culturally, European in the universal sense and English in the specific sense. For Deacon, the U.S. was the land of the "coon," and here we can recall what we learned in the last chapter about that creature in the popular imagination. In this regard, Deacon and Garvey were symbolically and metaphorically speaking the same language.

Deacon and his acolytes felt that Britain had betrayed Canada by sending "a steady stream of British immigrants [across] the Atlantic to build up the United States, to breed and be the parent of an undefined but very considerable proportion of the present population."[14] It had also sent human capital to India, to the colonies in Africa, and to South America, "where Indian and Negro blood is largely intermingled with white of the Spaniards." All these measures caused Canada's progress to be retarded.[15] "Where does Canada stand?" Deacon asked. And he answered, "By herself."[16]

In his description of the United States, Deacon painted stronger images, presenting Blacks as irresponsible, lazy, untrained, and untutored for freedom—views that were quite popular internationally, as can be seen in the writings of Thomas Carlyle in *The Nigger Question*. Most notably, Carlyle portrayed Blacks as irresponsible children who would be happy to live simply by picking fruits off the trees and vines, and who should for their own good be forced to work and be responsible. According to Deacon, the United States was also like an irresponsible child who had to be tutored. Canada was responsible, and therefore superior.

Deacon's views were not uncommon, thanks to the complete erasure from the prevailing imagination of three hundred years of Black presence in Canada. There had been a new beginning to Canadian history, and it was racialized. It did not recognize the presence of Blacks, and it repudiated the views of people like Simcoe. Instead, elite Canadians began talking about the founding fathers of Confederation, those who'd been party to the early search for a white homeland within the British Empire, in both Canada and South Africa. No Blacks, slaves or free, had memorials like those venerating the founders of Canada. Blacks were simply written out of Canadian history, and Lord Simcoe's legacy was suitably amended through an official whitewashing.

For Deacon, Canada's saving grace was that it had no Blacks and never did. It was not ethnically a Black country, unlike the United States. "Now the United States has one element we have not—the Negro," he said. "Their poet, Edgar Lee Masters, has pointed out that the only thing 'really American' is the 'coon.'" The United States, to Deacon, had started out European but become a place of miscegenation that had produced a mongrelized people, a subspecies of humanity called, pejoratively, "the coon." He wrote, "Everything they have is an importation from Europe except what is Negroid. Count [Hermann] Keyserling [the philosopher and spiritualist who founded the School of Wisdom and promoted unity between Western and non-Western cultures] has pithily phrased it: 'here you have a man [an American] with the body of a European, the manner of an African and the soul of an Indian.'

Starting with the music which, in its modern United States mani-festation, is distinctly negroid in tone and tempo; all that is distinc-tive about contemporary art of the United States is almost obviously Negroid in mood and inspiration."[17] Canada was not to be the land of the coon, an argument that had great impact on the dominant thinking about their country of elite Canadians. Such thoughts are even today found deep within the very notion of Canada and the Canadian identity (and that of its citizens), and even within what constitutes Canadian literature and culture.

Deacon had no doubt that the U.S. was destined to become another Haiti, both spiritually and temporally. This, he argued, was, in a Greek tragedy and biblical way, the curse inflicted by history on the United States of America, the natural home of the indigenous coon. And the tragic hero was complicit in its own downfall, which occurred when Africans had been forced to give free labour to the country. They might have built a country, but, typical of a master–slave relationship, they were also surrepti-tiously creating a culture that would eventually wrest that country from those who felt they were its natural owners. As the classical Greeks knew, the Fates were exacting and could not be avoided; the Furies of history were unforgiving in their attempts to restore, correct, and award justice; the Christian God would punish the unsaved and lift up the downtrodden and despised. "But it is a law of life that one may not labour for another without recompense," wrote Deacon, "and that spiritual law's inescapable punishment looms over the United States."[18] This was the same kind of natural law that governed the social orders that James Anthony Froude had warned about. It was the same kind of law of which Smuts spoke so glowingly.

The punishment of its degeneration into irresponsibility and social disorder was, Deacon argued, what made the United States distinct from Canada, a European country where the coon would be out of place. This was a modernization of the old Christian myth of the curse of Ham and his children, who were supposedly the Black man in this mythology. Whites in the United States had slept with the children of Ham and had become a peculiar race unto themselves. The members of the white race were destined to be punished for this contamination by the loss of their pristine whiteness. At the time Deacon was writing, one out of every seven Americans was Black, and he believed that Blacks were multiplying in numbers. According to him, the United States and Haiti, in their Blackness, were on a path of degeneracy, and each day would be worse than the last and each generation worse off than the previous one. But Canada, so European and white, was on the opposite trajectory—towards progress, development, and improving circumstances.

A well-read man, Deacon was drawing on a thread in the national narrative of the United States, a fear that someday the United States would have to pay in blood for the way it had treated Blacks and Africans. From America's earliest days, important men like Benjamin Franklin and Thomas Jefferson had argued that slavery had morally devalued their nation-state. "In Franklin's view," wrote Francis Adams and Barry Sanders in their book *Alienable Rights,* "not only did slave labor prove expensive but its presence seemed certain to diminish a nation. The white population of the Caribbean, he suggested, had been ruined by the introduction of blacks. The possibility of a harmonious, cooperative society in which everyone lived modest, upright lives—Franklin's ideal community—had been destroyed by the plantation system, which allowed a few to profit lavishly but left most people with little or nothing."[19]

For this reason, and because of the fear of degeneracy, Franklin changed towards the end of his life from a pro-slavery advocate to someone who was more sympathetic to Blacks and Africans. Jefferson also worried about the price that whites would have to pay someday for holding Blacks and Africans in slavery. This fear ultimately manifested itself in dominant whites keeping Blacks and Africans out of mainstream society—something that Adams and Sanders show can only cause consternation for African-Americans every President's Day holiday. After all, which presidents can they really hold up as genuine heroes for the African and Black cause? The politics of the United States, as exemplified by the Louisiana Purchase and its attendant political machinations, is the politics of race and, as some have suggested, the price of racism. This fear took physical form in the Haitian Revolution of 1804, an event that many white supremacists saw as the beginning of their extinction. The world seemed to them to be turning on its head, in a flash of natural or perverted justice, so that, as the English journalist Hesketh Prichard claimed, Blacks would rule not only other Blacks but whites too.[20]

Deacon saw the damnation that was already setting in as part of a downward social, political, and economic spiral. In the South, Deacon said, there were sections where Blacks owned every acre; they had penetrated businesses and the professions, and many were distinguished poets, musicians, and dramatists. Harlem in New York, with its six hundred thousand Negroes, was as big in population as the Toronto of his day. The result was a composite race of dark-skinned people, a culture and science that was of a Black civilization. In Deacon's world, this was a waste and a misuse of the gifts of Prometheus, and a situation that would get worse because, he said, "every day more and more white and black men and women are marrying each other. In time, the blending will be complete. Nothing can stop it."[21] Within a generation or two, he predicted, the United States would produce a new hybrid race, distinct in colour and homogeneous in culture, and this was the "coon" stereotype that even Garvey invoked to support his argument for a Black homeland. Indeed, Froude, Garvey, Deacon, and Smuts, among others, all invoked the same international symbol of this nationhood: the stars and stripes of the venerable U.S. flag.

The difference was that Garvey saw the flag as a symbol of prolonged Black oppression by whites, while those like Deacon saw it as a symbol of the growing dominance of the coon and of spreading miscegenation and cultural hybridization. As Garvey said, in the U.S. there was a joke that even the coon had a flag to symbolize citizenship, even if, in a practical sense, there was no such flag in existence. That same joke had resonance in Canada and South Africa, two of the supposed white Atlantic countries that were then presenting themselves as the last holdout against the advance of or encirclement by the coon—or, as he was called in South Africa, the Kaffir or Bantu.

Based on the trends he discerned, Deacon concluded that the dream of people like Garvey for a Black United States was in the process of occurring. But while Garvey expected this Black homeland to take shape in Africa, Deacon saw it evolving under the nose of Canadians, in the United States of America. "This means a Negroid United States in the not distant future, and a division not only of blood and culture, but also probably of language to a great extent," he wrote. "American slang is largely an African deposit upon the basic Anglo-Saxon." Already, he went on to say, there were signs in the United States that a national jargon was developing, and that there would gradually become visible two sets of manners and customs. In addition, time would produce two psychological make-ups that would be radically different on the north and south of the Canada–United States boundary—"a line far from imaginary now, but ultimately to be as well defined as the division between France and Germany—perhaps more so."

Faced with these developments, some older white families in the United States would have no option but to immigrate to Canada. Both Canada and these new families would benefit from this migration. The older families would enter an environment that would allow them to act maturely and to attain their highest ideal. For its part, Canada would receive more of the white immigrants that it so needed for its development, and these immigrants would bring "a certain gaiety we ourselves lack, a touch of abandon that will do us no harm, and a youthful zest and vigor we need." For the United States, nothing was likely to save it from an awful destiny for its historical shortcomings. It would be excluded from the white world. "There will exist south of us a people so much more child-like in their attitudes towards life that even if we should become irresponsible as the average white American of today—which we shall not—the national distinctions will still be as wide as, say, that between a contemporary white American and a Mexican."[22]

Deacon wanted to report as well on the order and bounty that were the results of wise choices, particularly those that made and kept Canada white. Indeed, because it was a European country, and therefore by nature more mature, Canada would have to provide leadership to the Americans. Here again, Canada was cast in the role of the elder and more responsible sibling. This would be necessary, particularly in business, to compensate for difficulties "as the crap-shooting Negro lends his personality increasingly to the guidance of the great trusts, banks and manufacturing concerns of the Republic."[23]

This was why Canada shunned such institutions as the Pan-American Congress, the forerunner to the Organization of American States (OAS), and became a member of the League of Nations, while the U.S. did not. "Canada is situated, geographically, in the Western Hemisphere," explained Deacon, "but the League of Nations we belong to has its offices in Europe because it is fundamentally a European league for world domination, and Canada has in the past identified itself with Europe."[24] This was what people like Smuts would have recommended for Canada. And, indeed, Deacon was right in anticipating Canada's foreign policy choices and priorities, because for decades Canada remained an anomaly—the only independent country in the Americas that refused to become a member of the OAS, a point marked by an empty chair that the organization's member states purposely placed at regional events. But Canada steadfastly and pointedly refused to accept the proffered membership, and the chair remained conspicuously empty for many years. It was not until 1972 that Canada agreed to accept observer status at the OAS, and then, in 1989, Prime Minister Brian Mulroney finally announced that membership in the regional body was "integral to Canada's interest." Canada officially became the thirty-third member of the world's oldest regional body in June 1991, when the foreign minister, Barbara McDougall, attended a council of ministers meeting in Santiago, Chile. McDougall said of the occasion, "I was welcomed with open arms by my Latin American colleagues. There was a general air of excitement at that meeting—first, because of the democratic ideals which every country now embraced, and second, because they were genuinely pleased that the 'other' North American chair was no longer empty."[25]

Looking ahead to the future, Deacon saw Canada growing in clout and size, and eventually taking over the role that a weakened and misguided Britain was abdicating. In Deacon's mind, the centre of real Englishness—the spirit that had produced the highest civilization—had shifted to Canada. In a strange way, Deacon had gone back to part of the original mythology of the American revolutionaries, who in seceding from Britain had claimed that the mother country had lost its way. England was no longer a fount of liberty; it was no longer the home of freedom, good government, and the highest forms of social order and civilization. Instead, it was corrupt and weak, and the protection of the ideals of liberalism had to be relocated to American soil. England was no longer capable of providing leadership and no longer worthy of allegiance.

Deacon was incorporating this European rebirth into the Canadian myth. For the revolutionaries and disloyalists, the coming of liberty to the Americas was a clean break with European history, but Deacon was commingling Loyalist and revolutionary mythology to support the creation of a white and illiberal Canada. He forgot, however, that the Loyalists who first came to Canada wanted to create a country in the image of their mythical England. In this way, and by ignoring the Black Loyalists and the slaves who accompanied the refugee Loyalists to Canada, Deacon was rewriting the mythology of the Americas to privilege a particular type of Englishness and whiteness. He had rewritten the myth so that it accounted for the prevailing Canadian imagery and its concepts of continuing European history. This made Canadians heirs to a legacy that, in a strange twist, amounted to a negation of the explanation that was first offered for the creation of a Canadian history and identity. It also was a negation of the path Canada was supposed to take back to the homeland, to the place where there was liberty, freedom, and social order. This was a refutation of an important component of Lord Simcoe's ideal for Canada.

This was a restatement of memory and the ability to recall. Memory had become refashionable and pliable: Deacon could mould and remould it as he wished. Lord Simcoe and others had believed that the United States would see the light and come to acknowledge the error of its revolutionary ways. After its period of withdrawal, it would then return to the order of the British Empire, not only chastened and wiser but changed as well. In one very important sense it would have been an America without slavery, an America in all logic constructed very much along the lines of revolutionary Haiti. But Deacon was presenting a myth that did not call for a return and did not call for a break in history. This myth started out with very clear ideals of who or what is Canadian—Europeans and those who are racially white. "Canada's destiny," he proclaimed, "is to carry to its logical peak the Aryan civilization of Europe." Deacon said that he expected that within a few generations Canada would be the epitome of what he called "the evolutionary accomplishments of a great race."

This race would be what would make Canada a white man's country. For this race of people would have "struggled more or less blindly, through millennia of toil and sorrow, to give expression to its intimate passion for intellectual development."[26]

Borrowing from Greek mythology, Deacon argued that Canada was the new Athens, a country of harmony, international goodwill and co-operation, and intellectual energy: a country at peace, rich and well governed. Deacon predicted that this country would be the envy of the world, a European nation-state that was independent in serene splendour. Canada would be the epitome of greatness, in general, and of European greatness, in particular—the highest achievement, as he saw it, of any of the purported human races. By then, the hapless United States, reduced to a virtual "coon" country with its attendant slack morals, would have recognized that it could have shared in this greatness had it not been for the War of Independence and the presence of so many Blacks. This realization would come, Deacon said, by the year 2000.

Even Deacon would have been surprised by the accuracy of his prediction. According to statistics from the U.S. census, whites will be a slim majority of 50.1 percent of the population by the year 2005. The United States has moved from being a country with a Black population of 10 percent to being a country in which non-whites—or Blacks, as people like Deacon, Froude, and Smuts would have called them—are in the majority. The only surprise for Deacon in the Census Bureau figures would have been that the threat against whiteness was coming not from people of African ancestry but from those called Hispanic. These are primarily people from the Spanish-speaking countries of Latin America, a significant number of whom have so-called Black blood because of cultural and biological hybridization. Deacon might also have been surprised to learn that Canada's non-European population rose to 13 percent in 2001, and might have been even higher if the 22 percent of Canadians who claim a mixed ethnic ancestry had been included. And yet neither country is the worse for wear. Indeed, both continue to prosper, according to just about every measurement of what Deacon and his like would have called development, progress, and civilization. Much good, it seems, has come from the evil Deacon had predicted.

SOME MIGHT QUESTION why so much attention should be paid to Deacon and his prophecy. Many, in fact, would dismiss him as a racist kook. But this is not the case. A lawyer by training, Deacon was a respected man of letters his entire life, and he was the subject of two biographies of significance.[27] As the literary theorists Clara Thomas and John Lennox note in their study of him, "when William Arthur Deacon retired as literary editor of *The Globe and Mail,* in 1960, he had been a full-time literary journalist for thirty-eight years—literary editor of *Saturday Night* from 1922 to 1928, of *The Mail and Empire* from 1928 to 1936, and of *The Globe and Mail* from 1936 to 1960."[28] These were powerful positions from which he helped to shape and create Canadian myths. An indication of his influence can be found in the letters published in the second biography, where he discussed with many of the top names of his time how to create a body of work that could be called Canadian literature. Some of the correspondence was with people who would make a name for themselves in Canadian literature; others would shape the literature through the publishing end and through the formulation of government policies. Deacon retired with great honour, perhaps in recognition that the state, as embodied in the people of the day, was willing to reward with praise and venerated memory his contributions to helping Canadians identify themselves and tell stories about their past and their possible future.

But it should be noted that Deacon's influence went beyond that of being the literary editor—no small feat in itself—at *The Globe and Mail.* His position at the traditionally Liberal paper gave him access to those in the halls of power, a holdover from the days when the paper's founder, anti-slavery activist George Brown, was the leader of the Liberal Party. Wilfrid Laurier and other Liberal prime ministers had valued the support and influence of *The Globe*. Laurier, for example, was on his way back from Washington in the company of the paper's editor when the Boer War broke out. The editor promptly advised him that he had no choice but to send Canadian troops into South Africa, which is exactly what Laurier did—over the vehement outcry of minority Quebecers. This was a position that Deacon supported as well.

Deacon was influential in other ways, especially through his work on *Saturday Night* magazine. *Saturday Night* took a point of view that was prevalent in Britain and throughout the empire at the turn of the past century and was promoted in such leading publications as *Fraser's* magazine in London. As Clara Thomas and John Lennox point out, the magazine was clearly racist in its attitudes. And we must remember that *Fraser's*, of course, was the literary mouthpiece of James Anthony Froude, and that he had used it to decry the North in the U.S. Civil War and to plead the case of the slave-owning South. Many publications in the British Empire, including *Saturday Night*, modelled themselves on *Fraser's*. In this case, imitation was indeed the sincerest form of flattery.

Deacon also had influence through his most famous book, *My Vision of Canada*, which, as Thomas and Lennox note, was well received by critics and the public alike. A Rabbi Eisendrath of Toronto was one of the few to break the salutary trend by expressing "serious concerns about its racist implications." According to Thomas and Lennox, "the book was the subject of several church sermons and a national radio broadcast at Thanksgiving, and by the end of the year Deacon was looking forward to the need for a second edition."[29] Because of the book, Deacon was adopted by the Native Sons of Canada, a pro-Canadian, anti-imperialist, predominantly Anglo-Saxon group that was middle-class and Protestant. By 1928, Native Sons had over one hundred assemblies and about thirty thousand members, and Deacon spoke at many of their gatherings. He would lecture on Canadian literature, and on the need for government to support the arts so as to build a distinctive Canadian identity and culture. When Deacon retired, at least four publishers were clamouring for his autobiography, an indication of how loved and cherished he was in some circles. The Canadian elites would continue to pay careful attention to his words and ideas well after his death.

Thomas and Lennox say rather apologetically that Deacon's book should be read as an exercise in idealism that showed the potential that was available to Canada, rather than purely as an exercise in history or political and social commentary. "Seen as a romance, however, as a dream vision and an exercise in fantasy wish-fulfilment, [*My Vision of Canada*] is immediately comprehensible. Its first part is concerned with dream, quest, and treasure and its last anticipates conflict or war, transformation, and final victory."[30] In their view, Deacon's book was an attempt not only to read history for a purpose but to give a singular meaning to the present and the future.

Others' views on Deacon differed from those of Thomas and Lennox. Indeed, Deacon was not the only intellectual or journalist to hold the views he offered. One of his contemporaries, Arthur Irwin, the former editor of the respected *Maclean's* magazine, often expressed similar opinions. In 1949, Irwin gave a speech in Buffalo, New York, that summed up his thoughts on what it is to be a Canadian. According to the February 1, 1950, issue of *Maclean's*, "The great interest aroused by his speech leads the editors to publish it here as his last staff contribution to the magazine."[31] Irwin told his audience that two things distinguished Canadians from Americans. "One: We are the northern North American with all that implies in terms of influence of climate and terrain on character and a way of life. Two: We are the unique American in that we alone, among the Americans of two continents, have insisted on maintaining political connection with our parent stem in Europe.... Only the Canadian American refused to break his political continuity with history."[32] Irwin's reading of history, and the differences in people and attitudes produced by it, was no different from Deacon's and his harking back to Athens and the sacking of Troy as the birthplace of democracy.

On leaving the magazine, Irwin became the commissioner of the National Film Board, and he was later appointed Canadian high commissioner to Australia and ambassador to Brazil and then Mexico. He eventually became the publisher of the *Victoria Daily Times* in British Columbia. So if it's true that Deacon's views are of a world based on the theosophy practised by him, then that world was not totally unique to him. In a sociological and phenomeno-logical way, his views flowed out of a specific culture unique to a commonly shared world.

In the end, Deacon's vision still haunts the Canadian imagination. To use a Socratic analogy, there were "truths" in his analysis, for by the year 2000 Blackness was firmly established as an important way of life in the United States. But we must never forget that in idealistic thought are contained the strains of hope and despair. Deacon and the elites of his time were at one intellectually with people like Smuts; all believed that the hope of the white world would mean despair for those classified as Black. We can even imagine Smuts, Garvey, Laurier, Mackenzie King, Froude, Deacon, and Irwin having a conversation across time about world affairs and agreeing to the importance of race to the past, present, and future of humanity.

While men like Deacon and Irwin dominated the national media and intellectual thought, there were others in the mix who painted a different experience of what it meant to live in Canada and held out hope for a different ending to Canadian history. One of these voices could be heard in the April 23, 1963, issue of *Maclean's,* in an article titled "A Black Man Talks about Race Prejudice in White Canada." The article was written by Austin

Clarke, a Barbadian immigrant who was coming to terms with his position in a country that was predominantly white. Clarke had at that time been living in the country for eight years. "This year," he wrote, "I became eligible for Canadian citizenship, but I do not intend to apply for it. Not because I undervalue this status, which is so highly prized by so many immigrants from all over the world, rather, because I do value its privileges highly, but realize that I would be accepting in theory a status that Canada does not intend to give me in practice—because I am a black man." Clarke said that because of the prejudice and discrimination he had faced in Canada, he wanted to remain a West Indian. He wanted, as a conscious choice and an act of freedom, to maintain a primary identity that implied all the superior ideals of humanity that Canada, in treating him as inferior, had tried to erase. Accepting Canadian citizenship, Clarke stated, was accepting that the Canadian view of him was correct: that he was inferior because of his Black skin and because he was born in Barbados. Still, Clarke held out the hope of someday becoming a Canadian citizen. "I do not expect to be given an executive job the day I become a citizen, but I would want and expect to find a job for which I am qualified—not a joe-job that no white Canadian with my qualifications would accept. I would not want to be pampered or be invited to apply for membership in the [exclusively white Toronto] Granite Club. But I would expect to be allowed to live in the degree of dignity which I earn and deserve: no more, no less."

Austin Chesterfield Clarke *did* become a Canadian citizen. And he did make a mark in keeping not only with his qualifications but with his talents. He became one of Canada's most prolific literary figures, winning accolades for himself and his adopted country at home and abroad. It all came together for Clarke in 2002, almost forty years after he first refused Canadian citizenship, when his novel *The Polished Hoe* won the prestigious Giller Prize for fiction and the Commonwealth Writers Prize. But by then, history had taken a course that the elites had not envisaged half a century earlier. Canadian citizenship had become more inclusive. It no longer differentiated between those who were genuinely Canadian and those who, as Clarke had suggested, were for all intents and purposes second- or third-class citizens. By then, the U.S. was viewed by elite Canadians not as a coon country but as the senior partner in an economically vital free trade area that was to be extended throughout the entire Americas, from the Antarctic to the Arctic. As we saw with the Organization of American States (OAS), Canada was no longer assumed to be an exclusively white country and therefore automatically superior to all others in the Americas. Immigrants had become the mainstay of Canadian population growth. Clarke might not have joined the Granite Club, but he did become a member of an even more exclusive group, the Order of Canada, the highest accolade Canadians can earn. History clearly had plans and a morality of its own, and this became obvious when spirit used someone like Austin Clarke to create an ending that was different from the one the dominant view had wanted and had fought to maintain. However, even in his finest hour, Clarke had to contend with acolytes of William Arthur Deacon and an image of Canada and Canadian culture—particularly its literature—that is European in the universal and white, racially and culturally, in the specific. Fortunately, what was once a majority view is now held only by an exotic minority clinging to historically discredited notions and ideals of Canada. The world had changed, but some legacies and ideals run deep and cannot be thoroughly erased. They simply lie dormant in the body. However, on the brighter side, Canada had become officially multicultural in purpose, and by accepting people from all parts of the globe as citizens, it has become the world in image and spirit.

IN JUNE 1990, the eyes of the world were once again on Canada. This time speculative history was being acted out in a grand ballroom at a convention centre on Toronto's lakeshore. The conquering heroes of racism and apartheid were among us. As a symbolic mark of Black history that year, the government of South Africa had finally released from prison the world's foremost freedom fighter. I sat in front of my television with my eldest son, who was only eight years old and not yet fully conscious of the significance of this event, and watched a moment of history—both an ending and a beginning—unfold. I felt I was participating in a historic moment. On the screen, we witnessed Nelson Mandela walking to freedom after forty years in prison for breaking the laws that were so prized by Smuts and others around the world. At his side was his wife, Winnie Mandela, who had advocated so strenuously for her husband's release. Finally, he and, symbolically, the Union of South Africa had both become free. Apartheid, as an official doctrine, was taking its last breaths. South Africa was collapsing not because it too freely entertained the mix of white and Black blood, as Smuts had predicted, but because it had *not* allowed such mixing. The foundation of South Africa, its ideology of whiteness and separateness, had been exposed by its own internal contradictions, and once the foundation began to shake the entire edifice collapsed.

The moment was palpable for Canadians too, for our country had been in the forefront of the fight against apartheid. As individuals, lawyers, members of religious organizations, government workers, and so on, Canadians had fought for this day of freedom. Canada had led the fight for the ouster from the Commonwealth of its erstwhile friend three decades earlier. It had played a prominent role in demanding that the United Nations impose economic and military sanctions against South Africa, and in perhaps one of its finest moments, it had placed human rights and the struggle against racism above ideology in the final days of apartheid, breaking ranks, under the leadership of Brian Mulroney, with the United States and Britain to demand that those sanctions be continued. It was Canada that fought for the release of Mandela from prison—

placing the country on the side of the angels of history but across the ideological gulf from President Ronald Reagan and Britain's Margaret Thatcher. Indeed, Nelson Mandela's freedom, and that of all those racialized as inferior and placed outside the South African nation-state, was sweet victory for all of us in Canada. After a long detour, our country had returned to the spirit of Simcoe in its international affairs and domestic politics.

Finally, in June 1990, the Canadian government had invited Mandela to visit the country to rest before he embarked on the remainder of his personal journey. This would involve leading his multi-racial African National Congress in the first free and democratic elections ever held in South Africa. Those elections, whose outcome was never in doubt, would make Mandela president of South Africa and start the official dismantling of all that Smuts and others of his time had established.

So it was as a president-in-waiting that Mandela came among us. The main event was the gala dinner at a hotel on the Toronto lakeshore. But somewhere along the way, the planners must have realized their dilemma. Something was not right about the list of prominent Canadians that organizers were using to decide who to invite. If they stuck to that list, one thing was certain: there would be virtually no Blacks in attendance. What would that say optically about Canada? Would the old guard in South Africa be able to point to the absence of Blacks as proof of the charge of hypocrisy they had for a long time levelled against Canada? What would this picture say to Black Canadians themselves about Canada? Canada was faced with the reality of an absented presence. Its promotion of multiculturalism at home and human rights and social justice abroad was in danger of being exposed as a fraud by its own internal contradictions. Could Canada explain this away? Or did it want Black Canadians represented at an event that, ultimately, was a celebration of the triumph of Blackness in Modernity?

On the day of the dinner, the message went out: Get some Black

Canadians to the gala. Blacks of all walks of life suddenly found themselves summoned to dine and commingle with the elites of the land. Sitting at my reporter's desk at *The Globe and Mail,* I received the summons from a friend of a friend who was connected to the federal government. His job was to seek out the requisite Blacks for the evening. With my summons came a request for the names of other prominent Black Canadians who could also be invited. That evening, I sat three tables away from the head table, positioned well enough to be constantly in the background for the television cameras recording the event. Many other mostly Toronto-based Black Canadians were also placed on show that evening. There we were, in full profile.

Never had so many of us found ourselves in such prominence in Canada before that moment—or since. And we celebrated. We did our country proud. We acted as if we were perfectly suited to such events, proudly welcoming to our country a man who looked just like us, though he'd had to spend so much of his time and energy on issues from which we'd reputedly escaped a long time ago. We joined with everyone in giving standing ovations. Those of us who knew them sang the words of the Canadian national anthem and shouted *"Nkosi Sikelel' iAfrika,"* the phrase that had been the international battlecry against apartheid and would be the opening of the new South African anthem. And we listened carefully to what Mandela had to say, for a part of us suspected that despite the myth of our escape to freedom so long ago, there were lessons to be learned from the struggle in South Africa that would be good for Blacks in Canada too. We were full Canadians—unhyphenated were we. We acted just as the rest of Canada expected us to, and for a moment not even the media recognized us as different from everyone else.

One thing I remember clearly. Prime Minister Mulroney, in introducing the honoured guest, pledged continued assistance from Canada for the reformation in South Africa, offering $5 million to the cause. Mandela, sensing the overabundance of goodwill, seized the moment as soon as the standing ovation had ended and thanked the prime minister for his generous gift of $5 million *American*. This, we thought, was a mistake in understanding on the honoured guest's part. So the chorus went up that it was $5 million *Canadian*. No, Mandela insisted, he had heard correctly. The pledge was for $5 million *American*. At this point, Prime Minister Mulroney had little choice but to concede. What the heck, he said, in the face of such negotiating skills, I may as well make it $5 million *American*. Canadian, American, Haitian, South African—what's the difference, spirit must have thought, when we are all Black? What the heck. But at that moment, Deacon and his followers must have rolled in their graves—for it had been their dream that the Canadian currency would be superior to the American.

Mandela thanked his host individually and Canadians collectively for the generosity. And he left the gala with a financial pledge that was worth about 30 percent more than intended. Years later, on another visit to Canada, he would retell this story fondly. "Canada is one of our best friends," he recalled. "When I came here in 1990, Brian Mulroney was prime minister at the time. Before I told him what I wanted, he got up and offered me five million dollars, and I knew he meant Canadian dollars. So I thanked the prime minister for giving me five million U.S. dollars, and that is what I got. All of us were happy." This story, he said, tells us a lot about Canada and Canadians. Indeed, it still does.

As someone both witnessing and participating in that event, I learned a great deal about Canada and about being a Black Canadian. I came away thinking that Mandela had taught us all a lesson about making the most of opportunities. For that one night, all Canadian Blacks imagined themselves as part of not only the international human family but the uniquely Canadian family as well. In a sense, Blacks and Canada had come a long way. On that one night, we were all on the mountaintop together.

It was good to be multicultural, to know that we were not excluded, pragmatically or otherwise.

Yet there is still a long way to go before such exalted views become common. One look at the demography of Black Canadians—what I call racial profiling by numbers—shows how far we still have to climb. According to the census, just over half a million Canadians, or less than 2 percent of the country's population, are Black. Most of us live in urban centres, with 47 percent in Toronto and its environs. Indeed, over 60 percent of Canada's Blacks live in Ontario and another 23 percent in the province of Quebec, with the majority in Montreal. Sizeable Black populations can also be found in Halifax and Edmonton. As a rule, the Black population is younger than the Canadian population as a whole. Children constitute a much higher percentage of the total Black population than on average.

"There are two and a half times as many elderly persons over the age of 65 in the total population than there are in the Black community," according to a report from the McGill Consortium for Ethnicity and Strategic Planning. "One implication of these findings is that the visibility of Blacks in Canada is heightened by the fact of having a larger percentage of young persons—who tend to be more visible generally than older people." A noteworthy point that the consortium did not raise, though it is one of the axioms of the social sciences, is that young people tend to be more visible in police and crime statistics, a feature that is now very much part of the discourse on the placement and role of Blacks in Canadian society. We'll return to this point shortly.

The census also revealed that there are substantially more women than men in the Black community, and that almost half of Black Canadians immigrated here in the past three decades, transforming the Canadian Black experience. "The centuries-rooted Canadian-born Black population is no longer the majority," concludes the McGill report. "Seven out of ten Black immigrants in Canada were born in the Caribbean. Apart from the Caribbean, 15 percent of the Black population was born in Africa and 10 percent in Latin America. Less than 2 percent of the Black population was born in the United States. Some other social characteristics tell the story of Blacks in Canadian society. Family structures are different from the norm: marriage is not as prevalent as in the wider society and about 40 percent of Black children live in single-family homes or in extended families with non-relatives by blood. The average for Canada, as a whole, is 15 percent of children living in such homes. The socio-economic characteristics for Black Canadians are of a mixed bag."

Levels of education are identical to those among non-Blacks, while fewer Blacks are unemployed or dependent on government assistance like welfare and disability payments. Blacks tend to have "substantially lower incomes" than non-Blacks, however, and they are less likely to be self-employed or to rely on investments for earnings. Blacks are also less likely to be found in senior management positions.

If self-determination is an indication of freedom in a society, then Blacks, who are less able to hire fellow Blacks or to make a living solely on their own, are not as free as those in the wider population. Blacks seek a higher level of social integration, for we must get along with others so that we ourselves can get along. "Almost 160,000 Black persons lived in poverty in 1991," the study found, "and they represented 31.5% of the Black population in Canada. Poverty rates for Canadians [especially among women] generally were dramatically lower. Only 15% of all Canadians lived below the poverty line in 1991—a percentage which is half that of the Black population."

But there is also another profile of the Black Canadian, one promoted by the news media. This is a picture of a group of people operating outside the bounds of society and living by the norms and codes of a different culture, and even a different civilization. They are still aboriginal to Canada and not fully part of the Canadian cultural landscape. They're different from the mainstream in their looks, actions, and thoughts, and are not often easily understood. Indeed, they are cultural barbarians at the gates. Or that is the picture that is presented when it comes to the issue of crime.

In recent years, Canada's major city, Toronto, has been in the grips of escalating concerns about violence associated with guns. Most of this unsocial activity is blamed on Black youths, with various newspaper columnists and city spokespeople describing the problem as gang-related. This is where the ideal of individualism that is at the heart of Modernity is taken to an extreme. Young people see themselves not as an integral part of society but as a separate unit that is adrift in a racial isolation from the larger social entity. The mainstream media and politicians have long been agonizing over how society can handle this apparent crisis that stems from the aberrant ideals of individualism. The issue took on added urgency when people began to be concerned with what they believed was escalating violence that, contrary to official statistics, was supposedly making the streets of the city unsafe. The media made matters worse by reporting on the supposed reluctance of Black Canadians to inform authorities on one another. In an absurd sense, it was as if young people and others in the so-called Black community had taken their individualism and their socially constructed collective identity to an extreme where they acted as if they were separate and apart; such a reality was frightening even to those who, in confirming this social construction in the media, were contributing to the community's resulting feelings of alienation.

These developments should not surprise us, for it is well known that a country is only as strong and united as its social capital, the depths of the trust its individual members share, and the covenant they have with one another. We see this collective trust and the willingness to protect a common social capital at work with our police officers and the men and women in the armed forces, who put their lives on the line in what is called altruistic suicide—where they agree to sacrifice themselves for others. This altruism is more prevalent when an individual is grounded in society. On the other hand, individuals are more vulnerable to the furies of destruction— forces that are harmful to them and to society in general—if they do not feel they have a lasting bond with the wider society. In those cases, they are more likely to commit anomic suicide—a term used by sociologists to describe the suicide of lonely, unattached people who see themselves as separate and apart from all others and have little or no social grounding.

Columnists from different newspapers make the same argument: Black youths belong to a culture that is different from that of the rest of Canada. Hundreds of them could be in the area of a brutal crime, yet none would co-operate with the police to bring the culprits to justice. But that is not the Canadian way, the columnists lament. Canadians are law-abiding and respect the police. They have a sense of justice that is in keeping with the need for good order in a civil society. Through their code of silence, and by not co(p)-operating with the police, Black youths are, in the minds of many mainstream Canadians, demonstrating that they are of a different culture. They are not yet Canadian, at least not in terms of their behaviour. These arguments imply that Black youths are aboriginal to the Canadian nation-state. These supposed social deviants are so unknowable to Canadians that when a local public radio broadcaster needed an expert for its town-hall discussion on crime and gangs, it had to find an American to explain a phenome-non that was nevertheless presented as clearly Canadian. What the heck, the argument seems to say, American, Haitian, Jamaican, Canadian—aren't they all the same if they're Black? And Black youth gangs are alleged to be such a common feature of the urban landscape in the United States and Jamaica that some Canadian elites thought that to get to the root causes of this evil, they should send the police chief of their largest city to visit these foreign lands and learn from the masters there. Yet perceptually, and in reality too, the problems remained in Canada and were of a Canadian hue.

These youths are positioned as outsiders. They have not consented to be part of society. They have not taken in the teachings of society, transforming its ethical norms into their own moral imperatives. When viewed from this perspective, these youths will be imagined as forever beyond the city walls. They are like barbarians speaking another language; they are a strange people dancing to what used to be called barbarous music. They are not as much Black Canadians as they are Jamaicans.

Yet this may give us the answer to our contradictions. These Black youths are not Jamaican or African-American but, symbolically, fully Haitian. For they are claiming a long legacy that includes majority rule and democracy based on equality, liberty, and fraternity. They are the heirs of the Haitian Revolution, and they believe that everyone enters society as an individual and then decides what, if any, groups to form. This is the thinking behind the majoritarian democracy of the one-man, one-vote system and majority rule. This is the struggle their ancestors fought in the Caribbean and Africa, where they sought nationhood based not on race and ethnicity but on the grounds that they were the majority and should, therefore, have power.

Democracies in the Caribbean and Africa are Black merely because that is the skin colour of the majority. It has little to do with specific cultures or ethnicities. But on arriving in North America, people from Black majoritarian societies found themselves confronted with a different kind of democracy. This is liberal democracy, and it is best seen in the United States, where a group of people called African-Americans were assumed to need protection—in the form of affirmative action programs, for example, and the redistribution of congressional seats—if they were to take their place fully in the nation-state. The idea was that the minority—as an individual or as a distinct group—had to be recognized. Canada is also officially a liberal democracy, which means that in the eyes of many, politics and social services are expected to reflect group affiliations.

Herein lies the problem, for Black youths are not liberal democrats but majoritarian democrats. These youths—like their parents and grandparents, coming to political maturity in the shadow of the Haitian Revolution—do not accept that society must protect specific positions for specific groups. They lament that they are always judged according to group norms, and that they are racialized instead of individualized. While they do accept group identities and share in group cultures, they also want the choice to be individuals who form a majority—and not one based on ideas of race, ethnicity, or special privileges. These youths want the right to be treated as individuals, to be free of ethnic and racial groupings. When they do not get these individual rights, they protest by refusing to conform to the scripts that have been handed them by a liberal democracy.

And contradictorily, when they protest, they do so in a group, even if in spirit they remain individualistic Haitian democrats. Even if they are called Jamaican, they have not yet become liberal democrats like the African-Americans whose behaviour and socialization they are expected to mimic. Their silence is like a cold shoulder offered to a society that does not want to include and accept them as individuals.

This analysis is missed in the hand-ringing that goes on in the Canadian news media. So is the idea that, ultimately, it is up to society to teach *all* its citizens its culture so that they become part of the general "they" that is the undifferentiated citizenry. The Black youth should be handed the same script as any other Canadian—one in which race does not matter and there are no naturally superior and inferior individuals in the society we are fashioning. And while it is true that all citizens must be willing to conform, society must also offer all its members a good and fitting reason to want to do that.

The rewards and incentives that some now enjoy must be offered to all. The privileges of citizenship must be shared by all. And one of the privileges that must be offered to Black youths is to be "imagined" as Canadian and to want to maintain this status. They must feel that it is in their greater interest to protect Canadian society, of which they are important and equal members. This notion of belonging, too, is missing from the reporting and analysis.

What we are dealing with are measurements of what I call the dream deficit. This is an attempt to quantify in real numbers, or perceptually, the experiences of being Black in a country that, ideal-istically, does not see the colour of its citizens. But I believe we should seek to see most distinctly the many colours in Canada, rather than trying to see none at all in some misguided approach to social justice based on colour-blindness. Indeed, what is the point of seeing the unity that is Canada if we are not going to accept distinctions and differences as the real brute facts of life? We should reaffirm these differences more fully, rather than trying to erase them into a colourless indeterminacy. The deficit is the amount of alienation that the individuals of a group feel when their lived experiences don't match up to their own aspirations, not to mention the goals society sets for all its members. This deficit is so much like the blank cheque and the insufficiency of citizenship of which Martin Luther King spoke. It is the lack that has to be filled so that individuals can become fully universal, when they can be at home in themselves and in the wider society. It is no different from the disappointments of the Black Loyalists at the beginning of Canadian national time.

As long as the dream deficit remains, there will always be ques-tions of race on the agenda. Even where there is a dream deficit for only one or two groups, the population as a whole has been racial-ized, categorized into superior citizens and inferior ones, first-class citizens and those of lower standing. Ultimately, the dream deficit is a measurement of acceptance and a sense of belonging.

WE HOLD THESE TRUTHS to be self-evident. This is one part of Modernity's promise. On the other side of this promise is *race* and its concrete expression, racism. Both these ideals—self-evident truths and race—spring from the same source, and each claims to be validated by laws and axioms. But somewhere in the middle is the lived condition, the planes where we act on faith alone. And in this place there are no self-evident truths, no unchangeable laws and axioms, and there is no way of neatly dividing people into clear and precise hierarchies. This is the problem that Modernity bequeathed us. This is a world of contradictions. And the only solution to contradiction that we have so far is faith, the belief that what we know is really the truth. Without faith, we remain tied in knots. There is no way out of human bondage and into a promised land. The mountaintop is significantly different from the planes below. In the lived conditions, as captured by our myths, we seem to be eternally wandering in the desert, or to be busily at work collecting and storing, but we never know if all that we have gathered up will be lost. This is the contradiction of the nation-state, where something that is imagined as good can often produce evil. Indeed, there is always the possibility that good and evil can issue from the same source.

Multiculturalism is the living out of faith, the belief that the good that humans choose will be a good not only for their times but for the future as well. But it does not pretend that today's good will be of any use tomorrow. This is where we differ in a significant way from many who went before us. We do not believe that we have found an unchanging good. Tomorrow, we realize, circumstances may change. We may discover that we were wrong; we may come to realize that solutions that seem essential right now are not good enough for the challenges of a new day. This is why faith is important; it's the belief that history will show that what we hold as true and good today will be found by others to be good and true for their times. Indeed, multiculturalism is the practised attempt to survive, rather than solve once and for all, the contradictions of life. It is a religion of negotiations, of living one day at a time, but it's also a hope that something better will come. In this respect, self-evident truths have a shelf life of only one day. Race and racism, by contrast, are the practising of history, the attempt to drag the memories and hopes of yesterday into tomorrow without subjecting them to the glare of today. Multiculturalism argues that self-evident truths often lack good and concrete evidence. They are merely hopes born of fear and despair. Multiculturalism is the hope that, indeed, humanity will reach the summit. And the symbol of a multicultural Canada is the wanderer and stranger of our mythology, the immigrant and refugee of our history. Migration and multiculturalism are both leaps of faith.

Yet they are also the basis on which Canada is building a Modern state and planning a future. Both immigration and multiculturalism symbolize that we know not what the future holds or who our fellow travellers will be. All we know with any certainty is that we exist, and that we must have had a past. But is it a past we can be proud of, or one we'd rather forget? The past need not be a predictor of the future. And the future can be like the past if we so choose. Multiculturalism and immigration allow us to live out the contradiction of a past that both does and does not matter while hoping for a future that may or may not be the same. Multiculturalism and immigration symbolize the belief that in the absence of self-evident truths, we can only hope for the good, and that the biggest obstacle to that good in the future will often be our unwillingness to acknowledge that, ethically, we are all still human, and that what we have created, even with the best of intentions, is never perfect but always flawed.

chapter four

HARVESTING THE HOPE OF HISTORY

A nd so we followed the two strands of idealistic human exis-tence to the point where they came together, or separated into nations, states, and race. The concern now is, Do they lead us back into the same dungeon from which we sought escape or forward to a time of hope? Do we continue to follow the strands into what appear to be social dead ends? One strand places us in a nation-state that's an exclusive homeland for a few of humanity's diversity. This would be the case for those who maintain positions of privilege within the nation-state. Another option is that of a nation-state that is radically universal and as diverse as humanity itself, a society that aims to be a reflection of humanity in its entirety, and a country in which all members of humanity are equal and share the same privileges and entitlements of citizenship. Dialectically, these paths have brought us to the current thinking that is best exemplified by Canada, a country that has imperfec-tions and has at different times adopted both methods as a route to what was thought as perfection.

One solution rests, perhaps, in seeing ourselves as poised at a very special moment of opportunity and creativity, a moment when we can be morally and ethically whole again. It is as if we are

returning figuratively to the source of all troubles and opportunities alike. Metaphorically, this would be the same as treating this
moment more as a point of departure than as a faithful continua-
tion of the past. It is a new beginning, imaginatively such as what
would have occurred before history started and before those
preceding us decided on a specific course of action aimed at
producing a specific type of people in a unique nation-state. This
time in starting over again, we would be armed with one thing that
we did not have before now. Ours would not be exactly a stab in
the dark, because we can benefit from the lessons of the various
histories that we have encountered.

This puts us in possession of knowledge that tells us what is good
and what is evil, and what can be harmful or beneficial to humanity. And one other thing we also learn is that history, as amoral as it
is, can at any moment turn against us again, just as it turned against
those who had to fight domestically and internationally against the
dismantling of the same racist and immoral nation-states that they
had had a leading role in building. We must remember that at a
significant point in history, Canada was on the leading edge of the
forces shaping Modernity. Back then, unfortunately, the country
tried to limit the expressiveness and creativity of the spirit of
Modernity. It tried to box it in. It had also tried to express
Modernity's wishes through a specific type of homeland that became
a prison for this restless spirit, which is always trying to extend limits
and reshape boundaries as part of its quest to be totally free.

Back then, Canadians tried to impose a purpose on this spirit
and to ascribe a specific aim and meaning to history in general.
Because of that, they found themselves at odds with a spirit of
humanity that had set for itself its own purpose and intent. This
spirit was extending limits and reshaping boundaries in its quest for
a freedom that is widely defined, with one gain leading only to
further and sometimes previously unthinkable demands for other
freedoms. This wide-ranging and non-specific quest for freedom

continues today, as we deal with the new challenges and opportunities of living in a multicultural country whose citizens are noted more for their diversity and differences than for their physical sameness. We must also deal with the challenges raised by instruments like the Charter of Rights and Freedoms, which we have put in place to ensure that we continue to respect and extend the freedoms that make us wholly human, whatever they may be.

There is something else history can teach us. It is that just as Canada had a pivotal leadership role globally in the past, one that took us down the wrong route into a racist nation-state, the country can once again claim a new leadership role, this time by embracing and extending and fully exploiting the good of the racelessness that is the promise and hope of multiculturalism. This is a new form of universalism that starts out being nationalistic.

By allowing ourselves to act as if we are in a new moment of creation, we show a willingness to let multiculturalism blossom fully on its own. If we stay on this path, we, like everyone else in the world, will always be living in a moment of faith, marked by the serendipity and magic of the moment. The present will always be an ecstatic revelry in the opportunity to create newness by mixing and matching peoples from all over the world without a specific plan or purpose—or at least none that is easily discernible to fallible humans. By allowing diversity and differences to continue to flourish, rather than artificially attempting to produce merely a sameness and a singular totalization from out of the multiplicity that is humanity, Canada indeed becomes a beacon to the rest of the world, just as Lord Simcoe had envisioned. This time, it would be a testament to the rest of the world of what is possible when humanity, in general, harvests hope for all, instead of offering hope to the few and despair and despondency to the many. This is a moment that is worth seizing before history moves on and lays low any other monuments that we may be building now according to a morality that is already rejected by time.

Today, having refuted earlier official narratives in its history, Canada is coming to terms with the realization that although its existence will always be flawed, it is possible for an entirely new and better Canada to rise up out of that imperfection. Once again, at the beginning of history, this new Canada would start out once more not with the despair of defeat and failure, not with a singular ideal to which everyone must conform, but with an open-ended hope and the wisdom that comes from knowing that race, as a way of categorizing people into exclusive groups, is evil. Canada starts out trying to preserve a radical moment of freedom, when within the dynamics of living are the limitless opportunities and choices that can occur only at a mythological beginning of time when nothing has yet been determined.

Like the lost children in the Grimm brothers' fairytale, we have followed a trail of breadcrumbs out of the dark forest to what we expect will be a new, more enlightened home. This notion of a return to the beginning is at the heart of the thinking on multiculturalism. It speaks to the idea of re-evaluating the past in terms of options that we believed we had at an earlier time and to determine if we made the best choices. By figuratively and even symbolically returning to our very beginning as social creatures, we are once again confronted with an array of choices and with having to determine if we should stick to the path we have always taken or branch out anew. Do we want the future to be similar to the past, or do we want a change? Do we want to be a creature of a particular history or do we want to start creating history anew, so that in the end it is as a people that we are created in history?

This is a utopian moment of idealism, but one that is different from those we've encountered in the dreams of the great men of Modernity. This time, we are not aiming for a static idealism, where life is fixed, everything is positioned as it should be, and there is no longer any opportunity for improvisation and creativity. In static idealism, we do not need to learn, experiment, or explore anymore; we have filled in all the blank spaces in our minds, and we know the essences and abilities of every person and thing. Static idealism is a utopia that is nothing more than a living hell. The new spirit of Modernity, by contrast, is fluid and unfixed, constantly changing and reformulating, and offering to all the freedom of simply becoming. This is the newness that makes us all shiny and optimistic; this is the hope that is always left in the box to comfort us in our darkest moments, when despair threatens to imprison. In this hope is freedom, and because of this freedom there is life.

We are also returning figuratively and ethically to a place where the difference is in ourselves, in the travellers who today are the immigrant and the refugee, the icons and symbols of radical universalism and freedom. We have the benefit of experience, and after the tragedies of the transatlantic slave trade, the Holocaust, and various genocides and killing fields in the name of ethnic purity and cleansing, racial certainty, and superior civilizations, we have agreed amongst ourselves on what is good and what is evil. We have found the place that we think offers us the best approach to securing freedom. It is a place where there are no races, per se— where no one group is more important than the others, and no one person is superior or inferior to another. In this place, I suggest, perhaps provocatively, that we return metaphorically to a seminal point in the mythology given to us by the three great monotheist religions of the world—Judaism, Christianity, and Islam. It is where, mythologically, we call our home Babel.

In the biblical story of Babel, human beings in all their tribes and diversity, but significantly speaking one common language and sharing a common knowledge, learn how to make bricks. They decide to "build ourselves a city, with a tower that reaches to the heavens, so that we may make a name for ourselves and not be scattered over the face of the whole earth. But the Lord came down to see the city and tower that the men were building. The Lord said, 'If as one people speaking the same language they have begun to do this, then nothing they plan to do will be impossible for them. Come, let us go down and confuse their language so that they will not understand each other.' So the Lord scattered them from there over all the earth, and they stopped building the city. That is why it is called Babel—because the Lord confused the language of the whole world. From there the Lord scattered them over the face of the whole earth."[1]

What I am suggesting is that we return to that city of knowledge in a new spirit, but this time without the hubris that so upset the Lord. We return in humility, fully cognizant that the conditions in which we live are what make us human. It is the existence that matters. It is our actions, as ethical markers, that will be different from those of our progenitors who were scattered from the original Babel. Our actions would not be an attempt to produce sameness by wiping out the differences between humanity and the gods, or between the rest of humanity and those who are privileged enough to ascend the stairway and be recognized as gods. This time, there is a return to this place of knowledge and to a gathering together of the scattered peoples of the world, but without an absolute intent, such as the plans to eventually see ourselves as transcending our human condition and becoming gods. This is part of the interpretation of the Babel myth in other religions, but in Christianity it is presented as the myth of punishment—of God confounding humans because of their pride.

But there is a general consensus, widely accepted as part of our daily attitudes and captured in such books as Susan Neiman's *Evil in Modern Thought,* that the Christian God is one of love and of reconciliation.[2] In the dominant Christian view, a loving and caring God would not inflict an evil on humanity for the sake of being evil, so there must be some good in what happened in the mythology of Babel. Some of this good is what we want to excavate and to hold up from that old city.

I am arguing that a significant part of that good is akin to what the British Rabbi Jonathan Sacks, speaking as an Orthodox Jew, has called "the dignity of difference," something I see at the heart of multiculturalism. Sacks challenges the great monotheistic religions of the world to look beyond their individual communities and their respective doctrines and to re-examine their notions of a God that supposedly made each of them only in His own image. If one religion says that only its members are the children of God, what does that say about those who are of a different faith? In this, Sacks asks a question that is as central to the discussion of multiculturalism as it is to religious and linguistic tolerance in what is now a global village—particularly one that through its diversity now assembles in most nation-states of the world.

To this end, Sacks suggests that a good starting point is the acceptance in Judaism that one does not have to be a Jew to serve God, and that people may choose different paths to the same end. He says, "This ancient [Hebrew] tradition has acquired new salience in a world threatened by civilizational clashes. It suggests that the proposition at the heart of monotheism is not what it has often been taken to be: one God, therefore one path to salvation. To the contrary, it is that *unity is worshipped in diversity*. The glory of the created world is its astonishing multiplicity: the thousands of different languages spoken by mankind, the proliferation of cultures, the sheer variety of imaginative expressions of the human spirits, in most of which, if we listen carefully, we will hear the voice of wisdom telling us something we need to know. That is what I mean by *the dignity of difference*."[3]

Nation building is an act of faith, no different from religion. Indeed, there is a long line of philosophical thought that suggests that the Modern state is the manifestation of a spirit that is the embodiment of this monotheistic God.[4] In inviting a re-evaluation of the myth of Babel, I am reminded of the same type of challenge that the philosopher Martin Heidegger gave to those searching for meaning in their lives and in the world in general. His suggestion was that there should be a metaphysical return so as to re-examine what had already been rejected. "We can, however, only prepare for dwelling in a locality by building," he wrote. "Such building may scarcely have in mind the erection of the house of God and of the dwelling places of mortals. It must be content with constructing the *road* which leads into the locality of the restoration of metaphysics and thereby permits a walk through the destined phase of an overcoming of nihilism."[5] We see some of this thinking in Pierre Elliott Trudeau's views on nation building, especially in his wishes for a strong, unified country that is noted for its diversity and in his belief in a just society. Multiculturalism captures the hope that a way will be found to overcome the meaninglessness of existence that is nihilism, the belief in our mythology that we are on the other side of God and are constructed in the image of nothing.

"I used to take religion very literally," Trudeau said in a reflective moment after he had left office. He was trying to explain his motivation for why he did what he did when he held the reins of power. Trudeau was thinking out of the dominant Christian theology and coming to terms with the role the Christian notion of justice can play in a rational and civil society in the here and now. "If God was God and Christ was his son, then certain things followed and you had to be quite strict in your beliefs and morals. But, as I began studying philosophy and theology, I had to confront the fundamental question of liberty. If God knows what is going to happen, does that mean you are programmed, predestined? Then I began to read Thomas Aquinas, who makes a distinction between the morals of a slave and the morals of a prince. A slave obeys the commandments of the Church because he has to, whereas a prince is the master of his soul and decides by himself what to obey. So, as a free man, I began to reinterpret some of the dogmas and ethics. I kept talking about freedom of choice and about conscience as the ultimate recourse for every human being. As a result, I was often thought more of a Protestant than a Catholic."[6]

And there is a reason for this almost religious approach to nation building. No nation, or people, is natural in the sense that it is absolutely unique, in that the people of the nation share nothing with the rest of humanity. No people, as a unit, is also so universal that its members do not have differences within their grouping—otherwise, contradictorily, they would just not be a people.

Without difference within the same polis or among its citizenry, as Aristotle indicated a long time ago, there would be no need for politics. And politics, whose idealistic aim is to produce the greatest good for all, is really all about the art of bringing unity out of diversity and difference. One of the main tasks for us in a multicultural era is to learn how to become a single people and still be as diversified and different as humanity itself. Indeed, as it is now trite to say, any nation-state can only be imaginary—it comes together in our heads or, as Sacks suggested, from "the sheer variety of imaginative expressions of the human spirits."

In our heads there can be unity in diversity; in our heads there can be difference in oneness. The art and challenge of politics is to make that unity in our heads the same as the one we live on a daily basis. With this thinking in mind, we can see the power in a metaphorical return to the land of Babel—a return where we try to maintain our humanity, which is our difference and diversity, and not eliminate those characteristics that make us truly human. We can see why, even in a Christian theodicy, the diversity of languages and cultures that God inflicted on humanity after the destruction of the tower was a precious gift to humanity, for it confirmed both our oneness as a diversified humanity and our separate, individual paths to a future without a specifically stated ending.

Now we need to let multiculturalism's natural spirit of humanity develop on its own and to allow the spirit, without interference, to manifest itself in the forms, faces, voices, and colours that it pleases. We, who so often misjudged ourselves as the main actors in this play of time, as the measure of everything instead of also the fodder of the ages, have the option of bringing ourselves in line with the place and its spirit, rather than placing ourselves beyond them. And like the gods we, mythologically, perceive ourselves to be, we can remake this place and its spirit into our own. In terms of time and the ability to make perpetual states, we, as humans, are the clay rather than the potter, for the states that we build not only will crumble with time but might be of very little use in terms of offering refuge to humanity.

In such a case, perhaps, we should view the state not as unchangeable and a maker of elite citizens but rather as a tool to be used by the citizens hoping to someday become elites. Here, in our idealism and hope, we will study war—and eugenics—no more. We should view this time and place as the mythological Babel, where we try to gather the dispersed peoples of the world together but are always failing. This is a Babel where everything by necessity comes in multiples (for that is the natural order)—histories, cultures, tongues, religions, complexions, and dreams. It's the prototypical multicultural state in all the ironies that such a concept implies as a Modernist thought. Pure forms and idols, if they do exist, may very well be multi-ethnic and multicultural if they are the aims to which we aspire. And we know that if the forms are diverse, then they can be pure only in thought. And they cannot have an essence.

As a particular home, Canada, this place and time to which we have come, is steeped in contradictions. We want a strong country that also privileges diversity. We want individual members to benefit fully from their virtues and talents, but we also want equality among all citizens. We want to be a people noted in the world for our humanity and good life, but at the same time we want to help all of humanity to achieve the standards that we enjoy. And within our boundaries, we want every individual, and every group, to be proud of his or her past but committed to a joint future that may even necessitate the repudiation of things in the past. We want to have the choice to self-identify as Canadians or as members of some ethnic group, but we demand universal acceptance and recognition of equality for everyone. Canada appears to be settling on the model that is multiculturalism, an official policy that is a synonym for contradictions and paradoxes; Canada has decided to live out its contradictions daily in the hope that problems of race and ethnicity will be solved tomorrow. Within multiculturalism, Canada finds not only an answer for its ideological contradictions but a model of hope that can be offered to all humanity. Socially, contradictions are as much the essence of hope as hope is the essence of freedom. Choices are what make us human, a condition that puts limits on our hopes and leaves us badly conflicted and tied in knots of contradictions.

"Every single person in Canada is now a member of a minority group," asserted the father of Canadian multiculturalism. Prime Minister Pierre Trudeau was tasked with holding together a nation-state that appeared ready to fracture into two distinct homelands. At the same time, he had to assure a growing number of immigrants from all the cultures and homelands of the world that they would find the advancement of their dreams in Canada. Out of many, Trudeau believed, could come one. Diversity and difference could be contained and maintained within a single unity. Contradictions did not always have to be solved. This was the philosophy and political economy that he gave to Canada, and to the world. "Freedom is the most important value of a just society," he said, "and the exercise of freedom its principal characteristic. Without these, a human being could not hope for true fulfillment—an individual in society could not realize his or her full potential. And deprived of its freedom, a people could not pursue its own destiny—the destiny that best suits its collective will to live."[7]

In making Canada officially a multicultural country that is a liberal democracy, Trudeau was reaching into the past for a univer-salizing strand that ran back through the famed Underground Railroad of Canadian mythology to Lord Simcoe at the start of this history. It is a journey of patience, and it thrives on endurance. Time will solve all problems if only in the long run we would all be dead, the mere fodder of history itself. Ours is simply to outlast the contradictions rather than fall prey to them. To this end, we are constantly negotiating and renegotiating with the tyrant. We are forever struggling to survive, and winning at this game is enough of an achievement. This was the reality that Canada had to confront as it aimed to become not a white man's country forever but a just society offering equity at home and abroad. The main plank is multiculturalism.

For multiculturalism, as a search for justice as freedom, rejects the notion of speeding on our way to a perfect ending in favour of carefully progressing towards a widely accepted goal, while constantly evaluating the progress and ensuring that the outcomes are as good as we intend. In this scenario, Canada would become virtually a history-less country defined by a single overarching narrative that is universally accepted by all who call themselves Canadians. To this effect, every day will signal another end of history and a new beginning in someone's narrative. Canada's greatness will be its future rather than its past. Its goal will be to create humans who are the best of all humanity, rather than the proposed perfection of the trait of a specific group or nation. These are qualities rather than forms of humanity. By emphasizing qualities, at one moment, Canada has de-essentialized identity as either ethnicity or race. Qualities do not adhere to categorizing boundaries, such as those marked off by specific human forms, for they are too universal to be contained in a single form or by a set of finite physical characteristics. Yet at another time, Canada privileges ethnicity, an implied essence of a smaller group within the Canadian body, as the solid foundation on which to build a unique identity.

In the end, Canada hopes to reconcile these contradictions, possibly by producing citizens steeped in certain common and admirable virtues but marked by their differences and diversity according to ethnicity. This, too, might be tantamount to squaring the circle, but the realization that it has yet not been done does not mean we should not make the attempt. And the knowledge that we rise to a new challenge does not mean that we are guaranteed success. Indeed, neither success nor futility will be guaranteed. We may have no more than an exhilarating journey that is living daily to the fullest. Only the trying, and the living, should be the guarantee we give to ourselves.

Canada would no longer have majorities and minorities, no racially superior and inferior citizens. A Canadian would be perfected not by physical or genetic characteristics but by social conditioning in the human values of compassion, understanding, and love. Canada would be not only for Canadians but for the world. This we can do by making the world figuratively *Canadian* in all its indeterminacy. What would matter most would be not the physical attributes of the individual but his or her human values. This is the promise of the Haitian model of the nation-state. Multiculturalism brings us right back to that from which we were fleeing. This is where the spirit has brought us. And paradoxically, the only people who seem readily to recognize this are some Canadian Black youths. They are the ones whose desire is for a fully majoritarian democracy in which every individual, regardless of group affiliation, is equally and fully a citizen. In this regard, these youths, who are presented as the epitome of the anti-social Canadian, can teach some of our media columnists something different about principles and about the human spirit of freedom.

Canadians would then be people who love the world as much as they love themselves. The world, in this case, would be found both within the Canadian nation-state and abroad. In terms of physical qualities and demographics, there would be very little difference between any random sampling of Canadians and any similar sample from the rest of the world. Such is the hope in our mythology. The main difference, however, would be the acculturation received in Canada. This would be a learning that banished race from the imagining of the nation-state. For in a revisited Babel, no races exist within humanity; race is the difference between gods who cannot die, and therefore cannot appreciate the human condition, and humans who do die, and therefore live the experiences of the human condition singularly and collectively.

We-the-people in Canada would be symbolically and politically the same as we-the-people of the world. And whether we assume a nationalistic identity or one that grounds us as members of the human family, we would all be uniformly free. Canada would not try to exist as one part free and the other enslaved; it will not look on the rest of humanity and see a part that is free and living in Canada and another part that is not free and is living practically everywhere else. Freedom, then, can triumph only if it wins out equally at home and abroad. Canadians expect their promissory note to be stamped "Fully paid, principle plus interest."

"Linguistically (and historically)," Trudeau said, "our origins are one-third English, one-third French, and one-third neither. We have no alternative but to be tolerant of one another's differences. Beyond the threshold of tolerance, however, we have countless opportunities to benefit from the riches and variety of a Canadian life which is the result of this broad mix. The fabric of Canadian society is as resilient as it is colourful. It is a multicultural society; it offers to every Canadian the opportunity to fulfil his or her actual instincts and to share those from other sources. This mosaic pattern, and the moderation which it includes and encourages, makes Canada a very special place."[8] Were it to fulfil this dream, Canada would be the place where race does not matter.

To achieve this dream, there is something in the dialectic of Trudeau's thought that still needs to be mined and excavated. When this is done, Canada will be so much closer to wiping out the dream deficit for all its citizens. The first vein is that notion of going "beyond the threshold of tolerance." For many Canadians, multiculturalism is an exercise in tolerance—one powerful minority conferring a subjective recognition on non-mainstream members. This offers no more than the old strand from history of a homeland ruled and occupied by a dominant group. In this we see the contradiction of one part free and one part slave disguised in the proposed unity. Every other group would be positioned according to the dominant group's blessings and goodwill. This explanation does not exhaust the contents and meanings of Trudeau's thought. Hence, we see that multiculturalism has to be more than mere tolerance of differences. It has to reach beyond the limits of our imagination, including even opportunities that we have not heard of or thought about.

There is still a surplus of meaning that cries out for notice. For as Trudeau suggested, Canada should be a country of minorities— all bondsmen and no lord, benevolent or otherwise. Therefore, there should not be a dominant group lording over all other minorities. Not if the country is also to be the liberal democracy that Trudeau intended, one where decisions are made by the majority but the rights and privileges of minority groups and individuals are protected, enshrined in the highest laws of the land, and not just tolerated. But remember, Canada is a country without a natural majority, which means that any majority has to be socially constructed. A majority has to express the wishes and the desires of the people—the people who are by nature minorities and in absolute terms mere individuals. What is hidden in this thought is the idea of universal equality, where all groups are minorities alike in power and social standing. They would all enter the nation-state with a prior claim only to minority positions, unlike people of earlier times, who used history, race, or ethnicity as claims to superiority in the nation-state. Minorities would be a majority *within* the state. This is another contradiction found in multiculturalism.

This presupposes a break in the hold of the dominant white gaze on multiculturalism—which is to say that multiculturalism and the state itself are not singularly for the benefit of a dominant group. Such a redefining of what it means to be multi-ethnic would lead to a time when, as Trudeau suggests, to be white is to be a member of an ethnicity or minority group like any other in Canada. Therefore, to be racialized Black and white would no longer be a projection of whites who are determining what boundaries should be placed on society and the different groups within it. This would be a society in which even those self-determined as white would have to renegotiate every day, just as all other groups do, for space and privileges above the minimum for all members of society (such as those enshrined in the Charter of Rights and Freedoms). Their claim on Canada would be as good and valid as the claim of any other minority group—but no more so. Their claim would have to be justified before and approved by the majority, formed out of all other minorities—as will the claims presented by any other group. No one starts the process with privilege.

This kind of radical equality, where one group's recognition comes from within itself and is not dependent on the tolerance of some stronger and more important group, is what we can call genuine multiculturalism. Genuine multiculturalism wipes out all prior claims and acknowledges only those presented by the parties. In this respect, the immigrant who is a Canadian citizen of one day's standing would have the same rights and privileges as any other citizen. This would include the right to negotiate a change in the existing social relations. This would include a valid claim to be heard and to be taken seriously, like any other Canadian.

And if the country is a democracy, the new immigrants will have clout to back their demands, power that has nothing to do with history in the country or previous social and political arrangements. Therefore, Canada would be eternally up for negotiation, with each new member having an equal say at the table. That the newcomers might be outvoted is an issue more of democracy than of structuring the country according to the longevity of claims. This is the new social relationship, where there can be no superior or inferior position. For in all our history, we are yet to find any group that rationally believes it is inferior and not the subject around which the world revolves. Such an approach to ethical living, more than anything else, destroys the bogus claim of race that it can determine scientifically and methodologically the superior from the inferior. And this view offers a radical interpretation of what multiculturalism really means, what it intends, even if those intentions are different from what it now delivers. The dream deficit still has to be eliminated. For, indeed, good and evil can flow from the same actions and dreams, and what makes something either good or evil might be no more than the perspective of the gaze.

Here we are, groping at an ecstatic moment of freedom in multiculturalism. This is a special moment, one that has been de-essentialized to rid it of the baggage of race. We will not hark back to an earlier time of greatness from which we have fallen and must now return. This is not the historical conservatism that we have witnessed in the Smuts and Garveys of this world. There is no harking back to essentialism or archetypes of idols and races. And we are not headed towards a specific, a homeland that is ours at the end of time—or even towards a new heaven, as Martin Luther King, Jr. and others would have had us believe. Instead, it is merely good enough and human enough to remain suspended in a moment in time somewhere between a beginning that we do not really know and an end of history that is beyond our control. This is to be shaped by a time that moves on while standing still. This is a new creationist and creative moment in multiculturalism— recognizing that we have been thrown into a world whose beginnings and endings we do not know and cannot control or predetermine. In this creative moment, we should enjoy the exhilaration of falling and leave the worrying until we hit bottom and, if we choose to, pull ourselves back up the mountain of our dreams.

The second vein that needs exploring in Trudeau's thought is that of sharing. A multicultural society, he said, offers to every Canadian the opportunity to fulfil her or his actual instincts and to share those from other sources. Much of the criticism of multiculturalism is that it leads from the path of social cohesion and a politically unitary state to social isolation, with individual ethnic majorities living unto themselves. This is the argument of the famed ethnic ghettoes. Much is made of Canada's Little Italys, Chinatowns, Little Portugals, and the like—these are the evidence of the confounding in a Babel that we want to go beyond, taking away what is good. These are supposedly representatives of Canadians living according to many different cultures. But this is not the full extent of the dream that is multiculturalism. For according to Trudeau, multi-culturalism offers opportunities for individuals to live according to the cultural instinct they have and know, but also to share these customs and practices with others. This suggests a two-way trade: members of one group sharing their culture with non-members, and equally a willingness by non-members to share as fully as they wish in a culture with which they are not familiar.

But in the end, all members of society will be sharing Canada's culture of sharing. This will be their main identity. What matters most is that no one is forced to live a life not in keeping with her or his dreams. Each person will be able to advance in society according to his or her own blueprint. As Trudeau argued, "Uniformity is neither desirable nor possible in a country the size of Canada. We should not even be able to agree upon the kind of Canadian to choose as a model, let alone persuade most people to emulate it. There are surely few policies potentially more disastrous for Canada than to tell all Canadians that they must be alike. There is no such thing as a model or ideal Canadian. What could be more absurd than the concept of an 'all-Canadian' boy or girl? A society which emphasises uniformity is one which creates intolerance and hate. A society which eulogizes the average citizen is one which breeds mediocrity. What the world should be seeking, and what we in Canada must continue to cherish, are not concepts of uniformity but human values: compassion, love, and understanding." Here again, Trudeau is challenging us to see the beauty at work in the unknown, in the indeterminate, in a Canada that fully exists only in the future.

When combined with the implications for multiculturalism as explained above, this is a fundamental break with the past, an approach that will possibly help us to manoeuvre around the different strands without coming to form a bigger problem. And this we may do by acknowledging that ours is a journey whose ending we do not know, except in a very general way. Ours is not an attempt to form an ethnic homeland. Ours is an attempt simply to exist together one day at a time, pushing back for as long as possible the need to bring the different strands together. Ours is playing in the dark and enjoying it just for the magic of playing and the mystery of what unscripted activities can produce. This kind of living is not dependent on knowing the neighbour's history or preferences. It is concerned only with daily living and with the social relations that allow us to live as neighbours and citizens. This does not stop us from dreaming that someday we will untangle every entanglement we encounter, but we will leave such grand designs until tomorrow.

Within this excavation of Trudeau's thought are the solutions to what, embedded in our independent interests and prior claims, might be viewed as an evil. If Canadians are constantly sharing their experiences, they will constantly be forming and reformulating what we may call the mainstream. Along with this new ethos would come new norms of conduct and expectations for individual and even group behaviour. In this way, specific groups will be moving in and out of the power circles through alliances and compromises, and by openly sharing the good and the bad of their existences. New consensuses would be constantly emerging, none outlasting its immediate usefulness before being overtaken by another. Within Trudeau's thought, we see dynamics of citizenship at work, and of unplanned, unstructured, and unanticipated outcomes that may even surprise us. They would be unplanned, unscripted, and effervescent. Indeed, the state would never be immortal or perpetual.

The bubbles of life that are analogously the multicultural mix would never let the state settle to the point of painting grey on grey. Seen from this vantage point, there is an element of immediacy in this arrangement, for there will be actions and outcomes that seem to spring forth on us, coming not necessarily as we would have thought but with a purpose and aim that was not premeditated or, on first appearances, even mediated. Such would be the spontaneity in the freedom of living. The intoxicant for this celebration of the living would be life itself. "Justice to me," explained Trudeau in one of his most idealistic moments, "is a warm spirit, born of tolerance and wisdom, present everywhere, ready to serve the highest purposes of rational man. To seek to create the just society must be amongst the highest of those human purposes. Because we are mortal and imperfect, it is a task we will never finish; no government or society ever will. But from our honest and ceaseless effort, we will draw strength and inspiration, we will discover new and better values, we will achieve an unprecedented level of human consciousness. On the never-ending road to perfect justice we'll, in other words, succeed in creating the most humane and compassionate society possible."[9] The rehabilitated Babel would exist only in our dreams. This is the metaphysical journey philosophers wrote about. History teaches us that all efforts to make it real are likely to fail, or to remain incomplete. Yet we are driven to try again—in the belief that there can be an end to history of our particular choosing, but that, meanwhile, it is the exercise of living and doing what is right that offers us the exhilaration of life.

This is the material of dreams—and not the wild-eyed stuff of day-dreams or utopian idealism, but the believing in a rationalized hope, born out of this approach to history, that will materialize into something positive. Until then, we will live in the shadow of the monuments we have built over history, all the while hoping that we have learned the lessons of morality from the past, and that we are now knowledgeable enough to discern what is good and bad and how we should treat one another.

AND SO WE ASK, Should we be thinking about a time that signals the end of Blackness? This question is posed so provocatively by the Black American journalist Debra J. Dickerson in her book *The End of Blackness*.[10] But almost immediately, we see its illogic, for as long as there is life, there must be Blackness. Blackness is eternal. It is the everlasting; it is that out of which came light and whiteness, and that into which they must return. It is time without end: the Blackness that gives whiteness life and takes it back in at the end. Indeed, rather than thinking of an end to Blackness, we should be anticipating and preparing for an end to whiteness—the true cause of race and racism. What most people who pose this question really want is an end to a projected Blackness, where in a racialized discourse all that is evil and slothful is cast onto a specific group. Projected Blackness is merely whiteness in disguise and hoping to be misrecognized. It is the trickster or evil genius at work. This, however, is not genuine Blackness. Rather, it is the occluding of Blackness, when white is painted over it in the hope of erasing the original. But with time, fresh paint will become weather-beaten and dingy, and a return to Blackness is almost inevitable. Blackness is eternal; whiteness is not.

Whiteness comes with its privileges, its elevations of one group over another and of one individual over all others. That is race. It is the separating out of what is considered to be not only the good but the preordained best, even before those qualities are put to the test. That, too, is race. What whiteness perceives it has left behind is the Blackness out of which it escaped. It believes that it has corrected nature, or that it has dominated it and has taken dominion over all that nature produces. Mythologically, this is the story of white Adam, who believes he is his own creator, who thinks he came out of nothing, who chooses not to be aware of where he comes from. Or, in the land of patriarchy, it is the whiteness of a Zeus-like being believing that out of his head sprung an Athena, the goddess of justice and of nation building, with the blueprints for how humanity should behave. To be mindful of Trudeau's reflection, this is a justice that is not socially constructed; it's presented as natural and seamless, as wholesome as if formulated by the gods. So whiteness presents itself as original and develops an ideology that stands the world and nature on their heads, and we are led to believe that the cause is the effect. This kind of projected Blackness is as illegitimate as a baby without a mother—ironically, something that is still the goal of some scientific minds. This Blackness is created by cloning whiteness—an Adam cheating death by reproducing himself in his own image, with an erased lineage and history.

Such thinking is foundational to the supposedly new order that whiteness strives to maintain at all cost, even by force and the enslavement of its mythological creator and the mother and father from whose wombs and loins it sprung. For as a select and supposedly enlightened group, fully in consciousness and knowing its many weaknesses and few strengths, whiteness knows that without such enslavement it would revert to Blackness if allowed enough time, and if the creative spirit that we call nature had its way.

Therefore, whiteness has to remain unnatural and at war with the seemingly corrupting forces of nature, which are always trying to rub out its unnaturally developed and supposedly pristine existences and civilizations. It has to be at war with the obsolescence that is naturally within its own body. Whiteness has to be at war with the Blackness that is both encircling it and also within. For this reason, if there is life there must be Blackness. And even if there is not a specific life, or way of life, there must still be Blackness. This, too, is a lesson from the Haitian Revolution: the replacement of the phoncy differences of the human-owning whiteman with Blackness, a plural and multicultural state where every person owns his- or herself, and where each person lives as freely as humans did before the arrival of a particular type of nation-state with imposed hierarchies and the beliefs that some people are inherently better than others.

Whiteness, like so many humans in the miscegenated Americas, knows that it is innately Black passing for white, and that, as is always the case, the truth will come out in time. Whiteness is a fight against nature, and the beginning of this fight was the beginning of the study of the unnatural, the imagined, and the perceived—of race and the war that is racism. Indeed, as so many philosophers have suggested, this imposition of limits to initiate this separation was the beginning of evil. And one of the first steps we must take to get back to the position that starts with the good is to jettison the notion that skin colour always matters as a way of classifying people. Skin colour matters only to those who have it and deem it to be important. That, too, is a lesson that was available to us at the start of Modernity, but it has taken us so long to begin to grasp it.

So whiteness, even in the minds of Black-skin thinkers like Dickerson, dreams of a time when history shall end, when time shall be no more, when the corruption in its body shall stop and it shall be released from the fear of being revealed as it really is: Black. Whiteness, therefore, hopes for a static utopia, one where it has achieved its ideals although the forces of time and creation are truncated and even stopped. Whiteness had long thought this static ideal to be the nation-state.

So maybe for us to return to Blackness, as a natural state for the good, will necessitate the denial and withering away of the nation-state as historically constructed as an exclusive domain for a specific race of humanity. Or it may require us to rethink the roles of the nation-state and ask ourselves if such an arrangement is the only means through which humans can become perfected, cultured, civilized, and progressive. Indeed, we may want to ponder a bit longer if to be civil is to be white, if being civil is the same as having a single citizenship in a nation-state. Or is it as Trudeau suggests—to have both minority and majority status; to be nationalistic and also a representative of all the others that are the rest of humanity; to be a particular and a universal; to be riddled with contradictions. So much, then, for the argument of thinkers like John Ralston Saul that we are at the end of global universalism.[11] Rather, such universalism is now captured as necessary and important, contradictorily, in the particular that is Canadian multiculturalism. An end to or collapse of globalism is the false trumpeting of yet another end to history.

Indeed, we may want to question much that we have long held sacred. We may now ask if it is possible to become fully human without first entering a state, or even if an entry into such an arrangement is necessary, if membership must be limited to one nation-state. Is this, then, the Blackness of citizenship that is always symbolized by the immigrant and the refugee, by the transnational and the sojourner, by an existence marked by impermanence and constant movement? Perhaps such fluidity and lack of fixity is the future of a world that knows its Blackness—a place where boundaries are not fixed for humans or capital, where sovereignty and responsibilities are negotiable and transferable from one living space to another, and where citizenship of a region, indeed of the globe, may not be as preposterous as it once sounded, and as it still sounds to those basking in their self-generated white light.

Typically, reasoning like this, in talking about an end to Blackness, is really arguing for race. Yet it is presented as a polemic against racism. Indeed, this type of discourse typically sets its sights on a particular kind of racism in which a specific group of Americans called Black extort goodness from another group of Americans called whites. The blackmail comes in the form of seeking redress for historical wrongs. Instead of helping those who claimed they were wronged, the extortion creates a dependency of Black on white and an enslavement of Black by fellow Blacks. To bring about reconciliation for years of wrongs, perceived wrongs, and wrongs imposed on the wrongs, Dickerson suggests a break in the current morass. There should be a new beginning, with the wronged of yesterday and the newly displeased of today ending their sniping.

This is the strongest point of her argument, and one that might appear enticing because of its appealing rhetoric and its cadence of African-American hip talk, trash talk, Black jiving, and at times even mere idle talk. For the pertinent question presumes the existence of a special race of people called Black. Note that these are not African-Americans, and they are certainly not metaphorical Haitians, in the sense of our earlier discussions. For in examining this end-of-history scenario, it is important to look at what is hidden away in the details—or in this case the footnotes. This is where we see who, in this universe, is really Black. "For our purposes, *blacks*," Dickerson writes, "are those Americans descended from Africans who were brought here involuntarily as slaves. This definition would include free blacks, even those who owned slaves. Immigrants of African descent, even if descended from South American or Caribbean slaves, are not included in this definition. *The End of Blackness* is specific to the American experience of slavery and its aftermath."

At least we are not being asked to follow the lead of so many students of *race* and equate Blackness solely with skin colour. But a definition like this is still problematic, for it intends to distil an essence out of what is often presented as an already pure essence of Blackness. So in this instance, Blackness is culture, and it is something called American. Therefore, if as is widely accepted there is no essence of Blackness on which race can be defined, at least there is still, as so many racists have long argued, culture. Difference of cultures is what now makes race definable. In this particularizing of culture, does Dickerson mean "American" as in the adjective that comes from the word "Americas," or what is called the Western Hemisphere? Or does she mean simply those sovereign states that broke away from the rest, came together in a Union, and called themselves the United States of America? A name can be so tricky. So that if Dickerson is really talking about America as a universal, how can she logically and rationally exclude those from the parts of the world that are called South America and the Caribbean?

And to take this one step further, can Dickerson be thinking of "American" as a unique lived experience, one that has a history, including one where many of the slaves who eventually ended up in the U.S. first stepped ashore in the Americas in the Caribbean and might have lived and populated parts of those islands before being moved on to the continent? In addition, does her definition of Black include the modern-day immigrant and refugee from continental Africa? These are troubling thoughts, for a definition that reduces Blacks to a special kind of native American would exclude all those whose parents were seamen who plied the waters of the Americas, setting into ports like New York, St. Louis, Portland, Vancouver, and Montreal, where they sowed their seed in the true sense of the word diaspora.

And perhaps most problematic would be that Blacks in the U.S., as a group, would not include the likes of Colin Powell, Malcolm X, Claude Mackay, and numerous blues, jazz, hip hop, gangsta rap entertainers. Indeed, going back further, what would we make of the seeming world citizen Equiano, or Gustavus Vassa the African, one of the first practitioners of the seminal African-American literature called the slave narrative? If this was her intention, then perhaps there *is* a need for an end to Blackness, and it should be replaced by African-Americanism. This definition is remarkable for another reason: it establishes race within a presumed race. It distils out some members of the presumptive African-American "race" and names them Black. Just as whiteness was, Blackness has been left behind on the way to achieving a higher level of whiteness that is African-American. Historically, what is here presented as Black the Haitian revolutionaries would equate to just another variation of whiteman.

To correct a perceived wrong against whites, some of us find it easy perceptually to do exactly what other race proponents have done before: create a subgroup called Blacks within an elite group in a wider universe called African-American, or manufacture a seeming subhuman species, those Blacks who are the poorer and illiterate cousins of the African-American, including those who came from other parts of the Americas. In either construction, it is hard to see the spirit of freedom inhabiting such bodies for long. The Haitian revolutionaries must be rolling in their graves over what has become of the universal quest for freedom and equal status for all peoples residing in the Americas.

These views and similar social constructions of Blacks occur in Canada and among those seen generally as ethnicized Blacks. The poet and academic George Elliott Clarke is one of the foremost proponents of this thinking. For him, the difference to be isolated in Blackness is mainly between those born in Canada and of several generations' standing (usually going back to the Black Loyalists or the early fugitive American slaves), and the newcomers and parvenus from the Caribbean.

In his collection of essays, *Odysseys Home,* Clarke writes, "I argue that African-Canadian culture and literature have domesticated—nationalized—their influences enough to create an aboriginal *blackness,* even if this mode of being remains difficult to define or categorize." Difficult indeed, if not impossible, especially without a clear answer to the questions, *Aboriginal* to what? Is it possible to construct an "aboriginal" status, or nature, within the state? Clarke puts the issue this way: "To speak about an 'African-Canadian' literature, then, I must be 'essentialist' enough to believe that an entity describable as 'African-Canadian' exists. ... In fact, I hold that African Canada is a conglomeration of many cultures, a spectrum of ethnicities. That perception colours the essays gathered here. For instance, the old, indigenous, African-Canadian communities ... of black Nova Scotian literature. The 'New Canadian' black communities, mainly of Caribbean origin ... Finally, the import of African American literature for African-Canadian literature ..."[12]

So an aboriginal, or indigenous, Black essence is made up of essences that have already been creolized and hybridized separately in the anglophone Caribbean, the francophone Caribbean, Nova

Scotia and elsewhere in Canada, and the United States of America—all supposed sites of essences that have been blended into a new, or *aboriginal*, Canadian essence. Clarke recognizes that the problem is his search for even a "modicum" of Black essence. "Given that *blackness* is so undefined and indefinable, one potential objection to my essays is that they group human beings on the specious—and spurious—grounds of shared 'race,' a matter of chance apportioning of pigmentation and melanin."[13] So true.

Still, Dickerson looks to this breaking of utopia as a time that will signal the arrival of a new and liberating day for Blacks, first as a community and then, if this liberation filters down, as individuals. This is not the type of liberation that was envisioned in Haiti two hundred years before Dickerson published her book. But perhaps Dickerson would argue that some people have the skin colour of the Haitian revolutionaries but not their spirit. She says, "The first step in freeing one another is for black people, collectively, to surrender. Blacks must consciously give up on achieving racial justice. They must counter any notion of achieving justice that is meant to even the historical score or to bring about full racial integration." The problem with integration is that whites think this is only an absence of tangible oppression. For Dickerson, it has not meant for whites a real willingness to educate children of all races together, nor has it meant the dismantling of inequalities that are part of the social structure. "What blacks must surrender," she argues, "is the notion that they can be made whole for the centuries of loss and the degradation they endured, that whites can be made to suffer guilt and shame equal to the portion they have dealt blacks, that white America will ever see itself the way its black citizens do. White America will never feel blacks' ambivalence for the Founding Fathers, it will never waver from nostalgia for that much-vaunted 'age of innocence' that the black experience alone proves never existed."[14]

Such is not the spirit. Perhaps what is needed by humanity in general—including all Americans, regardless of where they were born—is indeed a return mythologically to the age of innocence, a time before we got so terribly conflicted and confused. This was when all the world was Blackness, before God commanded there to be light and whiteness burst forth over the land. We can return figuratively to this place, and in so doing, we may want to cleanse our minds of what whiteness has taught us for the past three thousand years—and these are the lessons that are merely a projection of this whiteness. These lessons claim that in a racialized world, there are simply some people who embody all that is inferior, undesirable, unprogressive, and evil about humanity. These people have none of the attributes that would make them good and, incidentally, white.

The lessons told us that we shall know these peoples by the colours of their skins; the sizes of their heads, lips, and sexual organs; the languages they speak; their religions and sexuality; and any number of infinite characteristics than can be used to differentiate them from us. Those people, the lessons taught us, are simply Black. Perhaps the first step in this journey to liberation is for us to put an end to the whiteness that is a projection of a differentiating and racializing thought about the innate inferiority of some people, a lesson that even some Blacks have learned too well.

A second step would be to claim the legacy of the Haitian revolutionaries. Ultimately, they were fighting for the freedom of every individual, not for the acceptance of a specific group within a wider group. They were fighting for the recognition that the universe is peopled not so much by groups but by individuals who want to be free. Only once free can these individuals decide whether they want to form themselves into groups, and whether these groups should be white or Black.

But there is another way we can consider such a monumental change for this end to Blackness. It might indeed be possible to make a physical journey while being mindful of the American mythology about the highways to freedom. This would involve taking a closer look at the Underground Railroad and the North Star in North

American mythologies. These were the routes the slaves, often in their individual capacities, often leaving kith and kin behind, took to a land of freedom. This is the same place that Ishmael Reed wrote about in *Flight to Canada* and that the Nobel laureate Toni Morrison has referred to so subtly as the journey across the Ohio River and even further beyond. This place is indeed Canada, where official multiculturalism is trying to put an end not to Blackness but to whiteness.

This is the land imaginatively of Lord Simcoe. In the end, it is not even a question of whether Canada is more racist than the United States—or any other country, for that matter. What matters is the intent, the desire to do good while learning from history what is evil and taking every step possible not to repeat it. Alternatively, it is the lesson that says when we recognize and acknowledge an evil of our own making, we should abolish that evil, just as Lord Simcoe tried to do with slavery. Even more important than intent, therefore, are our actions—our ethical relations with one another as humans. But even then, Canada has not yet arrived in this Canaan of our mythology, where whiteness eventually had to take flight, leaving behind an officially multicultural land and intentions to do good to and for everyone.

WITH THE PRIVILEGES of old set aside, or more widely distributed, what can we look forward to? This is a question that seems to be at the heart of the multicultural country. In a sense, the answer is almost anticlimactic, for this is not a narrative that ends with high hopes or our arrival at some purported end of history. All the end tells us is that there is really no end, that each day is an end and also a beginning, and that this, too, is part of the diversity and difference of the human condition. So in a moment of different endings and beginnings, what can we hold on to?

Trudeau seemed to be suggesting that in times of fluidity, we can only hold on to our moral compass. This is what we take with us on our journey—indeed, as suggested in an old Negro spiritual, it might be the only thing we can take with us. This is not an exercise in relativism, however, where we get blown in every direction, depending on the strength of the gales we encounter in life. Our moral compass is based on our knowledge of past achievements and the lessons we've learned about what constitutes the human condition. In providing us with a moral compass, Trudeau was riding with us into a future that is not a specific and closed ending, where history supposedly completes itself, but an ending that is, contradictorily, really an "opening up"—an ending that is indeterminate, broad, and as inclusive as imaginable. This is the future of freedom that is also the freedom of the future, of a hope that is not absolute, and of living out our contradictions in good humour.

Trudeau hoped for a future that is rational but not rationed. It is to be based not solely on competition between those who are deemed to be deserving and those with lesser claims. It is to be based not on the privileging of some superior group over those who are somehow inferior. Rather, he called us to a future where we all have either the same superior claims based on a hope that is opened or an inferior claim based on historical notions of having already overcome and arrived. He hoped that we accept the first choice— a future that is open, that consists of the plenitude that is human creativity. This is a future where we do not worship or ascribe to ourselves an absolute image—this in our mythology is the curse or the evil of the mythological Babel, where humans arrogantly believe they possess the wisdom that can make them human no more. And we all know from our mythology or from psychoanalysis that our gods are archetypes of what we hold to be the best virtues of humanity. In this respect, the absolutes are humanity shorn of its inferiority—shorn of what is effectively our humanness. This is not genuine multiculturalism.

We are heirs to a legacy and guardians of the future. Yet we are all part of the same journey—one that was started by others in the past, that we take into the present, and that others in the future will finish for us and for those who went before. Yet those of us who are this intergenerational community have different parts to play. As Canadians in a moment that is the present, we recognize that those who started the journey in the past, perhaps because of a poorly developed or missing moral compass, made choices and decisions that many of us, once we'd acquired greater knowledge and wisdom, came to reject. Along the way, we took corrective action: we put in process the *en train* to take us on a different course. We, of the present, have to choose whether to continue the journey on this corrected path, or even to reverse and return to the old ways that were rejected. Another option is to stay on the path we're on but leave ourselves open to other possibilities. These choices are not opposites if we accept that when we corrected our path in the past, we chose to take a new road that meanders, allowing us to take our time as we ambled along, and that now leaves us open to new opportunities.

If we decide to continue on the corrected course that is multiculturalism, one of the challenges we face is how to deal with the privileges in our society that are a legacy of the old discredited way. When we talk about *race,* we are really talking about the power, privileges, rights, and entitlements of whiteness. Where do these not exist? In other words, can we transcend this whiteness here on earth, or is to do so merely to indulge ourselves in the unreal, the unpractical? Multiculturalism is an attempt to overcome and transcend whiteness in our time and through human effort. It is also an attempt to get more out of a morality, currently in vogue, that says it does not look good anymore to be seen benefiting from *race* gains. This is the case unless the gains—such as physical and financial property—were acquired many generations ago and have supposedly been cleansed by time, broken linkages, and amnesia, occluding any claims for reparations and the like. Ethically, we are always assuming that the rights and privileges of *race* will be eradicated in the future, and that it is proper and good for this to happen, maybe even in our children's generation, so that those who now enjoy superior rights may very well ask why they should not hold on for the present to the last of these claims to rights and privileges. Ethically, we will always be made whole and sound tomorrow. But this tomorrow of giving up privileges and entitlements will never really come, not unless there is a change in morality. In this case, this is where we do look forward to the end of a particular and nasty piece of history.

These are the privileges that give higher rights and entitlements in practice to those who claim a "superior" right. This claim is real and practical, even though we, as a society, have asserted that we will no longer honour such prior claims. They have become to us as blank cheques written on a fraudulent account, or as a cheque to be drawn on our account but not issued in the name of our new and morally improved society. We have said that as of now there will no longer be people with different rights, privileges, entitlements, and experiences of what it means to be a Canadian. However, that is still an ideal—it is not yet the lived experience of the day-to-day Canadian existence. Therefore, the present is indeed a mixture of the past, or what has gone before us, and the future, or what we hope for. In hoping for a multicultural Canada as a minimum, or a mere starting position, we must try, when we hand off the metaphorical baton to the next generation, to make the lived experience and reality as close as possible to what we hope will prevail at the end of our own individual race. Then those who come after us will have to decide what to make of multiculturalism as a place where *race* does not matter. We can only hope that they will regard it as a legacy worth keeping—that it is good to live in a time when everyone has equal privileges or none at all; a time when there are no claims to superiority or inferiority, and when the account that is our social capital is held in trust for everyone and everyone makes deposits through their labour and dreams.

But even here we may want to be mindful of the very language into which we have lapsed in trying to understand the intergenerational difference. Who is this next generation that is the "they" to our "us"? Indeed, just how is the present a mixing of the past and the future if "we" are not also the "they" of the next generation? For when does one generation stop and another begin? And is it not true that a significant part of the next generation is already with us, in all those babies who have been born in this moment and will come to maturity in what we consider to be the future? Equally, is it not true that the future generation will include significant numbers of people who do not now live in Canada or whose parents will have to be immigrants to Canada? In this case, what will be the connection between this future generation and not only ours but those that went before ours? With these questions, we will be engaging Modernity and its very ideals that indicate any of us is a single individual without any relatives in the past, present, or future. This way, we are fully challenging this notion of the subjective "I," or singular unity, that is so much the pride of Modernity.

Indeed, in the present, the future is already upon us, and some of the actions we are taking are in the name of an indeterminate future generation. The difference is that we, as Modernity's isolated egos, do not see ourselves in that future, just as some beneficiaries of the privileges of *race* claim no responsibility for the actions of others in the past. Yet in some areas, there is an unchangedness that seems to transcend generations. At a significant level, it is what we imagined as Canada. In many respects, we are validating decisions from the past and making them anew as much as if we were among those who first encountered the options. Similarly, we are also part of the next generation already. And it is for this reason that we need a strong moral compass that will allow us to move fluidly between these times. It is also for this reason that the future of Canada should not be closed off to what we can physically see or imagine, but should be kept open and wide enough to include all others—either the children of Canadians or those of other peoples who will be our immigrants, those Canadians who are not yet physically among us but are already part of the new spirit of Modernity and multiculturalism.

IN AN ANTICIPATED LAND of justice, the elements for a just society—where all men and women are free from racism and even racialization—are coming clearer into sight. For this reason, we see the hope that is contained in the dialectics of history and experience. And we dredge the bottoms of our idealism in the hope that what we discover will keep us grounded in a real world and shape our actions. There are still unresolved issues that are a legacy of our past and emerging ones that even now we can anticipate. We can face them, secure in a morality that comes out of our actions and experiences, and in an awareness of what it means to be, in the Haitian sense, Black and not a whiteman. Of concern to us should be whether as a society in general we continue to reap the benefits from a host of bills of rights and fundamental freedoms in Western society. Once there was a time when those of us with Black skins would applaud anyone like us who rose to a position of prominence within the nation-state.

As I write this section, I am aware of a landmark in my own life. This year marks a quarter-century since my arrival in Canada and the beginning of my process of becoming a Canadian. Hopefully, in the spirit of fluid utopianism and idealism, it is a process that has not yet ended. Still, I have a vantage point from which to look back. In twenty-five years, I have seen seemingly radical changes take place. Many of them came with a big fight. Many people paid a heavy price—some even with their lives, in the extreme that is physical death or a kind of social death that is the denial of dreams and aspirations. A generation of immigrants, for example, is moving into old age knowing that they will never attain the dreams they brought with them to this country, but that because of the sacrifice they made a later generation stands to benefit. This is the good with which they console themselves, the recompense for the evils of dashed personal dreams. Because of this, they can tell themselves that they made the right decision to leave their homeland to become a Canadian. Someday, they hope, Canada will fully understand the sacrifices of an immigrant, especially those who come from groups that, in the nethermost past of Canadian history, were deemed unsuitable for citizenship in a white man's country. Someday, someone will raise a monument to their long trek to full Canadian citizenship, and to the gains they have earned for themselves, their communities, and their nation-state. This monument will take its place alongside all the others that have already been dedicated. Someday, the non-white immigrant narratives will be incorporated as a significant and worthwhile part of the "real" Canadian stories, histories, and cultures.

Some of these earlier battles now seem mundane—fighting to get Black people to seek political nominations; to get them elected and in Cabinet; to see them among the happy citizens of the country, drinking beer on television, reporting the news, writing commentaries in newspapers, and hosting talk shows. We fought to see Black and other multi-coloured Canadians as firefighters, police officers, principals and professors, and soldiers dying for their country. Perhaps it is a mirage, but it seems as if we are fast approaching the point where we can claim, with Aristotle of old, that the best indication of full citizenship is the ability of an individual to hold office and thereby be fully involved in the governance of the state—in the governance, in other words, of him- or herself now and in the "colonizing" of the future. To be truly free. This is why we need to dream of the end to this specific journey, to see Black people living complete lives in their nation-state. For the first time in Modernity, it is possible to envisage the day when Blackness will be viewed as positively as the rest of humanity. So as not to miss an opportunity, we may want to look as deeply as possible into the mystic to see the mixing of the past with the present to produce the future.

Over the centuries, Blackness was associated racially with the negatives of humanity: instability and disruption, illiteracy, criminality, or primarily human instincts. As we look to the future, the negative stereotypes are still there, but there appears to be on the horizon a time when the negative typecasting will be automatically negated in our thinking by the positive attributes that have been withheld so far from those with Black skin. Put another way, in the spirit of equality, those with white skin will be assumed automatically to be capable of both negative and positive stereotypes. There will be no difference in the perceptions of those with Black and white skins. In the interim, people with Black skins are still achieving many social, political, and economic "firsts." Three things are now worthy of observation.

First, we know that old thoughts do not just die in society: the contradictions of life are simply overtaken by others, and the old ones remain under the surface offering any influence and even resistance that they can. No thought at any time is pure, for contained within it are elements from the past, some more dominant than others. Race and racism have been so deeply entrenched in our consciousness in Western thought that short of a social lobotomy—a revolution that paints anew how we view the world in radical gazes—it is unlikely that these two concepts will disappear from our daily lives. What is new is the realization that the current social consciousness has matured, and various provincial bills of rights and the federal Charter of Rights and Freedoms speak to this coming of age. Society has determined that it is in bad form to treat people in a racist manner. As a group, we have declared that racism is bad morally and ethically.

However, this does not mean that all individuals in wider society share this view, or even believe that it is the one that will ensure freedom for all of us. This may be a case where the general will of the universal group will have to force dissenters to see freedom with a different gaze to bring them in step with the rest of society. Indeed, it is extremely unlikely that in this social consciousness, we will ever be totally free of anti-Black racism, including, ironically, the variety known as Negritude, which argues that to have Black skin is to have superior characteristics. And of course, there is the more virulent strain of anti-Black racism, which posits all Blacks as inferior biologically and culturally and not fit for full incorporation into the Modern state. What we may be able to do is provide the social inoculation to limit any damage and to isolate this anti-social condition.

Second, even though people with Black skins still have social mountains to climb to receive recognition as full citizens, their achievements are becoming less and less noticeable as group accomplishments. They are personal. Once, Black and other minority people felt particularly burdened when they found themselves in pioneering roles, for they carried not only their individual and personal ambitions but supposedly those of their entire race. They were deemed to be a credit to their race, ever mindful they were likely to inflict great damage on their race if they failed. For they knew that they rose as individuals, setting the path for others like them to follow, but that they fell as a *race,* bringing all others down with them. In a place where there is no *race,* perhaps Blacks and other visible minorities will be released from their double burdens and their double consciousnesses.

We are already in an era when such "firsts" are both applauded and greeted with scepticism for having taken so long to occur. Today, the institutions and agencies of the state are routinely taken to task for not getting with the program sooner. Why, people wonder, did it take so long for such-and-such agency or institution to find someone with Black skin or a visible minority worthy of prominence? The fact that these institutions finally did find people is more an indictment of their lack of social awareness and good citizenship than testimony to the personal achievements of those they promoted.

Third, there are always truths in the stereotypes, although they limit those truths to finites instead of indicating merely a small part of humanity that is an infinite in opportunities and conditions. Our task is equally to liberate the stereotypes. Humility is needed now that we have "overcome" and the promised land is in sight. For questions will soon arise about how totally liberated people with Black skins really are. Would this mean that, semiotically, a Black skin would have no meaning or signification? Would there be nothing to preserve and carry forward if the culture eliminated *race* and racism? I want to answer that Black skin will always have meaning, and that there will always be memories to carry forward into another time. And in seeking what we should carry forward, it is again necessary for us to return to the mythologies at the beginning of our time.

Back then, as in the case with Greek and Hebrew mythology, there was something socially uplifting and meritorious about having Black skin. The Greeks tell a story of the destruction of the world by fire, which caused the natives of Africa to get Black skins. This happened when the sun came too near the earth, causing snowcaps to melt and deluges to happen. In Africa, it became so hot that deserts were formed and the blood of humans rose to the surface of their skin and boiled. They were Black because of the blood at the surface of their skin. Similarly, Hebrew tradition tells of the special mark of Blackness that was placed on Cain as he wandered the world looking for ways to establish lasting human settlements, or what would become nation-states. In all cases, the mark in these mythologies was black. It was a reminder of humanity, of the fragility of human life, and of the human need for a home that is safe and secure and protected. Black skin signified something important about the human condition.

This is the message that Black skin should still retain in a land where there is no *race*. This is the message of the trials by fire that humanity, in general, has come through, and of the hope that there can still be peace and prosperity for all in this world. Black skin would be a reminder to the entire world that we are *all* equally human, fragile, and fallible. And through their actions, those with Black skins—those who come from a line of racialized people who were always deemed by others to be descendants of slaves—will show that they have not become, in the Haitian sense, whitemen. Nor have they ever been coons. They will both look Black and act morally and ethically Black: they will bear the burden of reminding the rest of humanity of the dangers and catastrophes that can happen to all of us when we stop thinking of ourselves as humans and start acting as if we are gods. This will place a higher moral responsibility on all those Blacks who become national and international leaders and statespeople. It will be a burden for some, especially those with Black skins, to make sure that in their thinking and actions they do nothing that will place other humans in the slavery and social death from which they have escaped—that they do nothing to make others into coons, lesser beings, or just objects.

It becomes a responsibility, too. The little boys and girls of Martin Luther King's speech will have the obligation of living up to the high expectations of their ancestors, and those of all people who anticipate freedom for all and the enslaving of none, who fought to make sure that freedom was not only for a few but for everyone. Their responsibility, equally, is to hold the future faithfully and in trust for everyone. A higher level of morality and humility is expected—a higher level of love for the self through loving all humanity as much as the self. This way, as humans, we will be reclaiming a meaning and a memory that are as old as humanity itself. We will have a much better chance of overcoming that erstwhile dream deficit. For this is a meaning and a memory that is part of the dream to bring together the two irreconcilable strands of an idealistic human existence not in a knot of history but as a dream of hope.

NOTES

CHAPTER ONE: THE MORALITY OF HISTORY

1. Jan Smuts, *Towards a Better World* (New York: World Book, 1944), 104.

2. Ibid., 102.

3. Ibid., 97–98.

4. Marcus Garvey, *Marcus Garvey and the Vision of Africa,* ed. John Henrik Clarke (New York: Vintage Books, 1974), 285.

5. Ibid., 446.

6. Ibid., 296.

7. Ibid., 285.

8. Angus McLaren, *Our Own Master Race: Eugenics in Canada, 1885–1945* (Toronto: McClelland and Stewart, 1990).

9. Smuts, *Towards a Better World,* 116.

10. Ibid., 116–17.

11. Ibid., 6.

12. This is true even of First Nations groups. Much of their concern with the Canadian nation-state is that it would not uphold the treaty rights that establish a civil social relationship between Canada and its aboriginal peoples. It should be remembered that as the original peoples on that land that is now called Canada, aboriginals welcomed other peoples and shared what they had, before almost all that they had was taken away from them and they were no longer able to share.

13. James Anthony Froude, *Oceana: Or, England and Her Colonies* (London: Longmans, Green and Co., 1886), 7.

14. Ibid.

15. James Anthony Froude, *Two Lectures on South Africa* (London: Longmans, Green and Co., 1880), 2.

16. Froude, *Oceana,* 20.

17. Ibid., 25.

18. Ibid., 25–26.

19. Khushwant Singh, *A History of the Sikhs,* vol. 2, 1893–1964. As quoted in W. Peter Ward, *White Canada Forever: Popular Attitudes and Public Policy Towards Orientals in British Columbia* (Montreal: McGill-Queen's University Press, 1990), xx.

20. Hannah Arendt, "Expansion," in *The Portable Hannah Ardent,* ed. Peter Baehr (Harmondsworth: Penguin Books, 2000), 100.

21. Brian Douglas Tennyson, *Canadian Relations with South Africa: A Diplomatic History* (Washington: Universal Press of America, 1982), 25.

22. Ibid., 39.

23. Ibid.

24. André Siegfried, *The Race Question in Canada* (London: F. Nash, 1907).

25. W. K. Hancock and Jean Van Der Poel, eds., *Selections from the Smuts Papers,* vol. 2 (London: Cambridge University Press, 1966), 358.

26. Ibid., 374.

27. Ibid., 379.

28. These speeches were published in three annual collections by the Empire Club of Canada and can be retrieved on the Internet at www.empireclubfoundation.com/details.asp?SpeechI.

29. W. E. B. Du Bois, *The Souls of Black Folk* (New York: Modern Library Edition, 1996). On p. xxii of this book, he writes, "Herein lie buried many things which if read with patience may show the strange meaning of being black here at the dawn of the Twentieth Century. This meaning is not without interest to you, Gentle Reader; for the problem of the Twentieth Century is the problem of the color line."

30. Garvey, *Vision of Africa.* This collection contains a good summary of the disagreement between Garvey and Du Bois. It is worth noting that Garvey in particular had quite a following among Blacks in Canada, including many who petitioned the United States government on his behalf when he was imprisoned for mail fraud. It is also worth noting, as Rinaldo Walcott points out in *Black Like Who: Writing Black Canada* (Toronto: Insomniac Press, 1997) that the founding convention of the NAACP was held in Niagara Falls, Ontario, in 1905. Laurier most likely would have been aware of the growing Black consciousness movement. (Ironically, to make the founding meeting look authentically American, the U.S. side of Niagara Falls was painted over top of the Canadian background for the official picture of the occasion.)

31. Rayford Whittingham Logan, *The Diplomatic Relations of the United States with Haiti, 1776–1891* (Chapel Hill: University of Carolina Press, 1941), 110.

32. H. P. Davis, *Black Democracy: The Story of Haiti* (New York: Biblo and Tannen, 1967), 125.

33. Himani Bannerji, *The Dark Side of the Nation: Essays on Multiculturalism, Nationalism and Gender* (Toronto: Canadian Scholars Press, 2000).

34. Will Kymlicka and Magdalena Opalski, *Can Liberal Pluralism Be Exported?: Western Political Theory and Ethnic Relations in Eastern Europe* (Oxford: Oxford University Press, 2001).

CHAPTER TWO: THE BLACKEST MONTH

1. Donald Bogle, *Toms, Coons, Mulattoes, Mammies and Bucks: An Interpretive History of Blacks in American Films* (New York: Continuum, 1994), 8.

2. See the *Newsweek* issue of September 10, 2004, for a full report and an interview with Mandela in an article titled "Nelson Mandela: The United States of America Is a Threat to World Peace." Similar reports were carried on the BBC website, under the headline "Mandela Warns Bush on Iraq" (accessed on news.bbc.co.uk/1/hi/world/middle_east/2228971.stm), and CBSNews.com, under the headline "Mandela Slams Bush on Iraq" (accessed on www.cbs.com/stories/20003/01/30/iraq/mains538607.shtml). Also see the London-based *Guardian* newspaper of January 31, 2003, which carried an article headlined "Mandela Attacks Blair and Bush." That report says in part, "Nelson Mandela yesterday launched a withering attack on George Bush and Tony Blair, implying they were racists intent on war with Iraq and accusing Mr. Blair of abdicating his responsibility as prime minister to America."

3. Garvey, *Vision of Africa*, 303.

4. James Anthony Froude, *The English in the West Indies: Or, The Bow of Ulysses* (London: Longman, Green and Co., 1888), 342–43.

5. Ibid., 344–45.

6. Ibid., 287.

7. W. E. B. Du Bois, *The Philadelphia Negro: A Social Study* (New York: Benjamin Bloom, 1967), 5.

8. Ibid.

9. Ibid., xiv.

10. W. P. M. Kennedy and H. J. Schlosberg, *The Law and Customs of the South African Constitution* (London: Oxford University Press, 1935).

11. Ibid., 42–43.

12. Ibid., 44.

13. Ibid., 260.

14. Robert Borden, *Robert Laird Borden: His Memoirs* (Toronto: Macmillan, 1938).

15. Richard Veatch, *Canada and the League of Nations* (Toronto: University of Toronto Press, 1975), 91.

16. John Henry May, *The South African Constitution,* 3rd ed. (Cape Town: Juta and Co., Limited, 1955), 151.

17. Alan C. Cairns, *Citizen Plus: Aboriginal People and the Canadian State* (Vancouver: University of British Columbia Press, 2000), 25–26.

18. Stanley G. Grizzle, *My Name's Not George: The Story of the Brotherhood of Sleeping Car Porters in Canada* (Toronto: Umbrella Press, 1998), 102.

19. Robert MacGregor Dawson, *The Development of Dominion Status 1900–1936* (London: Frank Cass and Co. Ltd., 1965), 281.

20. E. S. Reddy, "United Nations and Apartheid—A Chronology" (New York: United Nations Centre against Apartheid). Accessed at www.anc.org.za/un/un-chron.html.

CHAPTER THREE: MOUNTAINTOPS, VALLEYS, AND MULTICULTURALISM

1. All quotes from Smuts in this chapter are from his collection of speeches, *Towards a Better World*.

2. John W. Dafoe, *Canada: An American Nation* (New York: Columbia University Press, 1935), 28.

3. In 1780, Pennsylvania became the first U.S. state to abolish slavery, albeit for newborns only. It was followed by Connecticut and Rhode Island in 1784, New York in 1785, and New Jersey in 1786. Massachusetts abolished slavery through a judicial decision in 1783. From a timeline of Black history, accessed at www.timelines.ws/subjects/Black_History.html.

4. From a conversation with the African historian Prof. Paul Lovejoy, head of the Nigeria Hinterland Project at York University in Toronto, Canada.

5. W. L. Morton, *The Canadian Identity* (Toronto: University of Toronto Press, 1961), 3.

6. John A. Schutz, "Joseph Galloway's Historical and Political Reflection," in *The Colonial Legacy*, vol. 1, *Loyalist Historians*, ed. Lawrence H. Leder (New York: Harper and Row, 1971).

7. Ibid., 60.

8. James W. St. G. Walker, *The Black Loyalists: The Search for a Promised Land in Nova Scotia and Sierra Leone 1783–1870* (Toronto: University of Toronto Press, 1992), 11.

9. Ibid., 2.

10. Ibid., 73.

11. Ibid., 85.

12. William Arthur Deacon, *My Vision of Canada* (Toronto: Ontario Publishing Company, 1933), 1.

13. Ibid., 4.

14. Ibid., 77.

15. Ibid., 84.

16. Ibid., 88.

17. Ibid., 118.

18. Ibid.

19. Francis D. Adams and Barry Sanders, *Alienable Rights: The Exclusion of African Americans in a White Man's Land, 1619–2000* (New York: HarperCollins, 2003), 26.

20. Hesketh Prichard, *Where Black Rules White: A Journey across and about Hayti* (New York: Books for Libraries Press, 1971).

21. Deacon, *My Vision of Canada*, 119.

22. Ibid., 121–22.

23. Ibid., 122.

24. Ibid., 126.

25. Barbara McDougall, Opening remarks to the conference on "Diplomatic Departures?: The Conservative Era in Canadian Foreign Policy, 1984–1993," Hull, Quebec, November 18–20, 1999. Accessed at www.ciia.org.speech3.htm.

26. Deacon, *My Vision of Canada*, 252.

27. Clara Thomas and John Lennox, *William Arthur Deacon: A Canadian Literary Life* (Toronto: University of Toronto Press, 1982); and John Lennox and Lacombe Micheele, eds., *Dear Bill: The Correspondence of William Arthur Deacon* (Toronto: University of Toronto Press, 1988).

28. Thomas and Lennox, *William Arthur Deacon*, 2.

29. Ibid., 183.

30. Ibid., 179–80.

31. *Maclean's, Canada in the Fifties: From the Archives of Maclean's* (Toronto: Viking, 1999), 131–39.

32. Ibid., 132.

33. Halder, "Rising to the Challenge," The e.peak, issue 5, Vol. 100, www.peak.sfu.ca/the-peak/98-3/issue5/rising.html

CHAPTER FOUR: HARVESTING THE HOPE OF HISTORY

1. Genesis 11:1–9.

2. Susan Neiman, *Evil in Modern Thought: An Alternative History of Philosophy* (Princeton, NJ: Princeton University Press, 2004).

3. Jonathan Sacks, *The Dignity of Difference: How to Avoid the Clash of Civilizations,* rev. ed. (London: Continuum, 2003), 20–21.

4. G. W. F. Hegel, *Phenomenology of Spirit* (Oxford: Oxford University Press, 1977).

5. Martin Heidegger, *The Question of Being* (New York: Twayne Publishers, 1958), 103–105.

6. Pierre Elliott Trudeau, *The Essential Trudeau,* ed. Ron Graham (Toronto: McClelland and Stewart, 1998), 2.

7. Ibid., 16.

8. Ibid., 145.

9. Ibid., 19–20.

10. Debra J. Dickerson, *The End of Blackness: Returning the Souls of Black Folk to Their Rightful Owners* (New York: Pantheon Books, 2004).

11. John Ralston Saul, "The Collapse of Globalism and the Rebirth of Nationalism," *Harper's,* March 2004, 33–44.

12. George Elliott Clarke, *Odysseys Home: Mapping African-Canadian Literature* (Toronto: University of Toronto Press, 2002), 14.

13. Ibid., 16.

14. Dickerson, *End of Blackness,* 16–17.

ACKNOWLEDGMENTS

There are many people who have been part of the conversations that helped my thinking in this book. In many respects, this book is a conversation that ranges over time and will continue after—I hope, because of—this book. Many of the participants are outside of Canada, and I have met them only through their writings. Even though I do not mention all of them by name, they will be recognized when encountered. To them all, I give my thanks.

But in Canada, my cup overflowed, for indeed it is good to be in the land of the Underground Railroad, where the phrase "a friend among friends" has a special and historic meaning. Chief among my friends and mentors is Howard Adelman. I am greatly indebted to him and have learned much from him. Howard was the supervisor for my dissertation at York University, and he has had an immense influence on me. I suspect that those who know Howard well will hear his voice at several points in this book, and that they will even at times hear Howard strongly opposing what I am saying. Hopefully, the latter will not be too frequent. But hearing his strong and wise voice is one of the joys of being a student and friend of Professor Adelman—that and the fact that any conversation, once begun, never really ends. In addition, I would like to thank Les Jacobs and Alan Simmons, both professors at York University as well, for allowing me the opportunity to discuss many of these ideas with them. One other person whose conversations, both in person and in his work, also inform my work is Will Kymlicka of Queen's University, arguably the top academic worldwide on multiculturalism. Undoubtedly, these academics and friends will disagree with some of the things I am saying, but they will always be part of the conversation.

Significantly, this is also a conversation with all the academics and intellectuals studying Blackness and multiculturalism in Canada. These are people with whom I have had conversations as individuals, in groups, and through their works. I have learned a lot from each of them, and they all have my admiration. Among them are Austin Clarke, Prof. Rinaldo Walcott, Prof. George Elliott Clarke, Dionne Brand, Prof. Carl James, Prof. Nigel Thomas, Prof. Wesley Chrichlow, Prof. Leslie Sanders, Prof. Agnes Calliste, Prof. George Sefa Dei, Makeda Silvera, Prof. David Trotman, Prof. Andy Knight, Prof. Patrick Taylor, Prof. Ato Sekyi-Otu, Prof. Paul Idahosa, Prof. Paul Lovejoy, Prof. David Divine, Prof. Arnold Itwaru, Prof. Afua Cooper, Prof. Sherene Rezack, Prof. David Chariandy, Prof. Ratiba Hadj-Moussa, Burnley (Rocky) Jones, Munyonzwe Hemelaga, Roger Rowe, Dr. Yvonne Bobb-Smith, Gus Wedderburn, Bill Downey, Dr. Horace Goddard, Aaron Kamugisha, and especially, Dr. Winston Husbands, Dr. Sheldon Taylor, and Mayann Francis, executive director and chief executive officer of the Nova Scotia Human Rights Commission. May the conversations between us continue in the name of scholarship and friendship.

In addition, I want to thank my colleagues at the University of Guelph, particularly Femi Kolapa in the Department of History, Thomas King in the Department of English, Joubert Satyre in the Department of Languages and Literatures, and Richard Phidd in the Department of Political Science. I am also indebted to my colleagues in the Department of Sociology and Anthropology—particularly Tony Winson, Hans Bakker, Ken Menzies, Terisa Turner, Martha Rohatynskyj, and Belinda Leach—and to Pat Case of the University of Guelph's Human Rights and Equity Office. Needless to say, while I take much from friends and colleagues, they are blameless for any errors and misunderstandings on my part.

One other thing is a personal pleasure: this book allowed me to work once again with a very special and thoughtfully curious editor, Ed Carson. Ed is also the president of Penguin (Canada). But from this writer's narrow perspective, Ed is, first and foremost, an editor *par excellence*. All my major works in fiction and non-fiction—from my first novel, *No Man in the House*, to my most noticed non-fiction book, *A Place Called Heaven: The Meaning of Being Black in Canada*—came about directly under Ed's guidance. I give thanks to Ed, even though he keeps telling me that good editors stay in the background. Well, not this time. Similarly, I wish to thank Catherine Dorton at Penguin for the care she extended to this book and Janice Weaver for her careful editing. In a similar light, I also want to thank the people at the Westwood Creative Artists agency, particularly Bruce Westwood and Natasha Daneman, for all their encouragement.

Finally, to all those who at a personal level are so near and dear to me, and who help me to take the highs in stride and to survive the lows: I want to thank my three sons, Munzie, Michello, and Mensah. Truly you are the best gifts I have ever received, and I love you all dearly. Raphael and Christene, you, too, are precious gifts, and you both complete my family. And my *speego*, Orville Folkes, the truest friend I have ever had. And to all my relatives—particularly my two elder brothers, Stephen and Errol—in Barbados, Canada, England, United States, and elsewhere: I thank God for all of you, and most of all for Sharon, whose love makes it all possible, who has read and re-read with great care every single draft, and who blesses my life with happiness every day.

INDEX